*of related interest*

**Asperger's Syndrome**
**A Guide for Parents and Professionals**
*Tony Attwood*
*Foreword by Lorna Wing*
ISBN 1 85302 577 1

**Pretending to be Normal**
**Living with Asperger's Syndrome**
*Liane Holliday-Willey*
*Foreword by Tony Attwood*
ISBN 1 85302 749 9

**Asperger Syndrome in the Family**
**Redefining Normal**
*Liane Holliday Willey*
*Foreword by Pamela B. Tanguay*
ISBN 185302 873 8

# An Asperger Marriage

*Chris and Gisela Slater-Walker*

*Foreword by Tony Attwood*

Jessica Kingsley Publishers
London and Philadelphia

First published in the United Kingdom in 2002
by Jessica Kingsley Publishers Ltd
116 Pentonville Road
London N1 9JB, England
and
325 Chestnut Street
Philadelphia, PA 19106, USA

*www.jkp.com*

**Library of Congress Cataloging in Publication Data**
A CIP catalog record for this book is available from the Library of Congress

**British Library Cataloguing in Publication Data**
A CIP catalogue record for this book is available from the British Library

ISBN 1 84310 017 7

Printed and Bound in Great Britain by
Athenaeum Press, Gateshead, Tyne and Wear

# Contents

# Foreword

An adult with Asperger Syndrome can develop a successful relationship with a life-long partner. This statement could once have been considered as fantasy, especially as the person with Asperger Syndrome and their parents may have had some doubts during their childhood that they would ever have a genuine friend, let alone an intimate relationship. When one considers the diagnostic criteria for Asperger Syndrome, clinicians may also doubt that this can be a reality. However, one must recognize several key factors inherent in people with Asperger Syndrome and their partner. The person with Asperger Syndrome can gradually acquire relationship skills by intellect rather than intuition, especially if they have motivation and guidance in the areas of friendship and relationships. Their partner identifies endearing characteristics of being gentle, reliable and vulnerable and provides tuition in interpersonal skills. As the person with Asperger Syndrome matures they can successfully camouflage their social difficulties to their colleagues and acquaintances. However, their family and especially their partner can be aware of significant difficulties in perceiving subtle social cues and knowing the expected response. Unfortunately the achievement of an intimate relationship is at some personal cost both to the person with Asperger in terms of the mental effort required to maintain the relationship and to their partner in having to change their expectations of the relationship. This book is the first to examine a successful marriage from both

perspectives and provides knowledge that will be of value, not only
to similar couples and individuals with Asperger's Syndrome who
are considering a relationship, but also the organizations that
support relationships.

When one reads Chris's description of the marriage there could
be some initial doubt that he has Asperger Syndrome. His descriptions include an insight and self-reflection that would not be
expected when one considers the characteristics of the syndrome.
One must remember that while such individuals have considerable
difficulty converting their thoughts into speech, there can be a
remarkable eloquence when expressing their thoughts and feelings
with written language. I have met and corresponded with Gisela
and Chris over several years and have no doubt that they have an
'Asperger marriage'.

The relationship has provided mutual benefits and as Chris has
written 'I think I could not have found anyone better for me personally'. It is not only fortunate for Gisela and Chris that they met,
it is fortunate for others that they are prepared to disclose their
intimate feelings and experiences in order to help other couples
achieve a successful relationship.

The authors discuss their concerns and particular issues, especially the mutual misinterpretation of actions or, more often, lack of
actions. This can be due to not reading or understanding the signals
or context and the tendency for those with Asperger Syndrome to
do nothing in order to avoid making a mistake or evoking emotions
that are confusing. Chris is able to explain how he has achieved
progress with his understanding of social situations, but some of his
success is undoubtedly attributable to Gisela's guidance. People
with Asperger Syndrome tend to be detached individuals, reluctant
to take advice and preferring to retreat into solitude when stressed
or considering a problem. Chris has gone some way towards
changing this aspect of Asperger Syndrome and to consider and

benefit from Gisela's thoughts and knowledge. Gisela has also admired his talents, particularly in Information Technology and languages as well as his determination to make the marriage work and to be a good father to their son. They are better as partners than individuals.

The authors also discuss the changes in mood and the difficulty in expressing and managing emotions that characterise Asperger Syndrome. In particular Chris is prone to be melancholy and anxious. He describes his anxiety in social situations and how he feels 'more than slightly downcast for a majority of the time'. Where once 'ignorance was bliss' his insights into being socially clumsy have replaced ignorance with despair and anxiety. As he is gradually becoming more able to read the thoughts and feelings of others, particularly Gisela, and knows what to do in specific situations, Gisela has also become more aware of Chris's thoughts and feelings and to understand why he may respond in a particular way. There has been an emergence of mutual understanding and respect. The knowledge and strategies acquired by Gisela and Chris have strengthened their relationship and this book will strengthen other relationships.

*Tony Attwood*
*December 2001*

# Acknowledgements

I would like to thank the following for all their support over the years of our marriage.

- Chris's parents for all their wonderful help; they are not just my parents-in-law, but very valued friends.
- My children, Hugh, Henry and Olivia for their great senses of humour and understanding.
- Poonam White for her friendship and also for her careful reading of the draft of the book.

All my friends, both on and off the autistic spectrum, on the ASPIRES Internet list for their insight and encouragement.

*– Gisela*

# 1

# Introduction

## *Gisela*

When I told my mother-in-law the title of the book, *An Asperger Marriage*, her reaction was immediate and totally unexpected; she was upset and said 'Oh, surely there is some affection there'. I couldn't understand her response until she repeated the title she had misheard back to me: *An Iceberg Marriage.*

Sadly, I am sure that there are some people who meet my husband Chris who suspect that an 'iceberg marriage' would be an appropriate description for a marriage in which he is a partner, but fortunately this is far from true.

This book is about our 'Asperger marriage'. We are not speaking for anyone else, though I am sure that many couples in a similar relationship will recognise some of the issues raised as being almost identical to their own. I would like to be able to say that the issues, including marriage, of adults with Asperger Syndrome are well documented, but that is not the case. Like many other couples in our situation, we have met with the view that people with Asperger Syndrome do not get married. Fortunately, the majority of professionals in the field of autism now acknowledge that people with Asperger Syndrome do indeed get married and it seems that they have a higher tendency to produce children on the autistic spectrum. However, this book is not an epidemiological work, nor is it a general guide to 'Asperger marriages'; it is our own personal experience of our own 'Asperger marriage'.

For many women (Asperger Syndrome is much more common in men than women), the diagnosis of Asperger Syndrome in their marriage has followed years of unhappiness in which their husband's behaviour had been eccentric to say the least and, in many cases, the marriage has been irreparably damaged.

When Chris first received his diagnosis, I found little solace in the literature that I read from other women in a similar situation. I sensed a great deal of bitterness and could understand, given their experiences, why they felt the way they did. Although I could identify with some of the experiences myself, I had revisited them in my mind and seen that I had misconstrued Chris's actions or, more usually, lack of actions or words.

It is worth remembering that just as any two people who do *not* have Asperger Syndrome are not the same, no two people with Asperger Syndrome are the same. They do, of course, share a number of characteristics that enable them to be identified as being on the same autistic spectrum. Also, as they say, 'It takes two to tango', and my presence in the marriage is just as influential on its uniqueness as Chris's. We are a couple and we both can influence the success or failure of the relationship.

# 2

# Terminology

## *Gisela*

This book is not addressed to a particular audience, but I am assuming that many readers may have Asperger Syndrome themselves, have a family member who has Asperger Syndrome or be professionals with an interest in autistic spectrum disorders.

As terminology can be an emotive issue, I have decided to explain the reasons for using the terminology we have used in this book.

Asperger Syndrome is now regarded as being an autistic spectrum disorder (ASD). For those people working with Kanner type autism (the more severe end of the autistic spectrum), it can be difficult to see Asperger Syndrome as a disability in those who apparently have managed to acquire an education, employment, partner and children.

Some people with Asperger Syndrome are content with the way they are and do not feel that they are adversely affected; on the contrary they are able to value the gifts that this syndrome can bring. On the other hand, Chris described himself as 'socially handicapped' even before the possibility of any diagnosis had been entertained. Asperger Syndrome has materially affected all parts of his life: progress at work, in education, choice of career and job, social life and, of course, our marriage.

The appendix of the National Disability Council's *Code of Practice* in relation to the Disability Discrimination Act 1995 (United Kingdom) provides explanations of what is regarded as a disability under the terms of the Act. 'A person has a disability if he has a physical or mental impairment which has a substantial and long-term adverse effect on his ability to carry out normal day-to-day activities.' The capacities that can be affected include 'memory or ability to concentrate, learn or understand'. The main difficulty in accepting the term 'disability' for someone who is intellectually able is that people generally perceive the terms 'learning disability' and 'intellectual impairment' as being synonymous. However, particularly in terms of employment, Chris is discriminated against the moment he agrees to attend an interview. The stress of an interview is heightened by the fact that it is a situation that is heavily weighted against the person with Asperger Syndrome (AS). For this reason alone it is worth using the term 'disabled', and we apologise to those readers who are uncomfortable with this.

Increased awareness of autistic spectrum disorders has led to the diagnosis of AS in adults. There is also an increasing emphasis on the necessity of 'good communication skills' in every aspect of life from education (speaking and listening in the English orders of the National Curriculum) to 'more rewarding' personal relationships and employment, and this has made life more difficult for the person who might once have been regarded as an eccentric or the Victorian father (or mother) who locked himself away in his study or took off to the pub every night to drink away her wages.

Paradoxically, in the twenty-first century it seems that those who pride themselves on their ability to communicate are less accepting of those who, by definition, find empathy difficult. To me, this suggests that they also have deficiencies in communication, but as they are in the majority they are not seen as 'disabled'. How then to describe those people who do not have AS? For the purposes of this book, I have avoided the increasingly popular term 'neuro-typical (NT)' not least because I am not 'NT' myself as I have epilepsy, and so the term 'non-Asperger Syndrome' has been used throughout.

# 3

# Relationships

## *Chris*

I'm sure that just thinking about potential relationships occupies a significant part of most teenagers' lives, and for sure this was true for me, particularly so, given that all of my secondary education was spent at a boys' boarding school, where as you can imagine there was a lot of talk and (mostly) speculation about the opposite sex. Since most teenage boys' talk is more hot air than fact, which I realised at the time, and given the fact that most of the talk came from the same small handful of boys, I didn't expect to meet 'the right girl' through one of the usual channels, which for us usually meant one of the discos which were organised fairly often by my school or one of its local associated schools (there were two girls' schools within walking distance).

Indeed, I felt that this ideal partner wouldn't be the sort who would frequent such events. This leads to some fairly obvious difficulties, namely that there seemed to be no alternative means of coming into contact with anyone whose interests lay in directions other than the mainstream. However, I was usually hopeful that 'something' would happen to move things along.

Television programmes thrive on marital discord but I wanted to make sure that I wouldn't fall into any of the poor behaviour that seemed to dominate many relationships and which to me seemed absolutely needless, like the casual unpleasantness, stubbornness, unwillingness to compromise, etc. This intention set me apart from my peers, who made at least a show of thinking only of themselves. I always thought that I could be faultlessly reasonable; needless to say, my reality hasn't always lived up to this expectation!

I never had any clear idea about exactly how I would meet someone appropriate, and I was very conscious of the perceived fact that 'people like me' tend to keep themselves apart from the general interaction which enables meetings to take place. This of course could lead to frustration, and it wasn't always easy to remain optimistic about it, but in general I always thought 'something would happen' without having any clear idea of what it would be.

This may give the impression that I had definite ideas about the particular qualities and characteristics my ideal partner would possess, but this was not the case. Nevertheless, I think I was realistic enough to realise that the peak of physical perfection wasn't a reflection of the real world, and so I was more certain that mental and intellectual characteristics would be more important. (Since then my ideas about what is more physically attractive have become clearer, but that's a different story.) I found the idea of a series of short-term relationships uncomfortable, because that would have meant going through the whole process of meeting and getting to know someone time and time again, and so I wanted as far as possible to establish a lasting relationship with someone who was my intellectual equal, who would be able to hold her own in most situations and who would be a good listener and a friendly adviser, not on any specific subjects, but who would be intelligent and reasonable enough to make at least an informed guess at just about anything.

Every teenage boy I knew secretly harboured elevated opinions about his hidden depths and I was no different in this respect. Indeed it was exactly that – hidden depths – that I thought were just waiting to be discovered. It turns out now in later life that those hidden depths are nothing but a kind of universal *angst* about life, the world and everything in general, which more than one friend has told me is not unique to me. (This is very difficult to describe in words because it's such a diffuse and elusive kind of feeling, like a far-off and uncertain threat, but I can imagine that it might be quite common amongst people with AS.) Still, I felt that there would be a woman out there somewhere who would find me attractive because the quiet ones have hidden depths.

To make it clear, I was no less interested in the opposite sex than anyone else of my age. However, beyond that, my interests diverged. Besides the usual Asperger-type things I was about the only person I knew who was interested in classical music, and although I was sure that there must be at least a few girls of a similar age who would have at least that much in common with me, it was not made easy for me to meet them. This isn't an indictment against a lack of cultural development provided by the average English independent school, because there were regular organised events of this sort, but probably indicates a lack of imagination on my part.

I know that there is a current opinion amongst some of the professional Asperger-studying community that people with AS don't get married. Yes, I have been told this to my face by one such professional. This seems to defy all logic. There is an even more common opinion that AS has a strong genetic component, and if AS people never reproduce, then this genetic component would have died out at an early evolutionary stage, when in fact diagnosis is becoming ever more common. By making this point I want to talk about the relationships with girls and women that I have managed to have, and how they came about.

I was fortunate enough to go on a week-long school visit to the Soviet Union (as it then was), which took in the cities of Leningrad (now St Petersburg) and Moscow. Quite by chance there was a girls' school following exactly the same itinerary as us (in those days the official Soviet tourist agency made sure they knew where everyone was all the time) and I suppose that they were as interested in us as we were in them; this never went beyond a few days' terrible teenage groping which was fuelled by easy access to alcohol and each other. Besides that, I remember that week as one in which I seemed to be a different person from my usual self, and, more importantly, I think that my school compatriots seemed to be different as well; everyone was more relaxed and open and in fact more accepting, so much so that I didn't have that sense of having to look over my shoulder all the time which I shall describe elsewhere. Anyway, despite the fact that I wrote one of the girls a letter once we had all gone back to school, I never had a reply and that was as far as it went. And I can't even remember her name.

Timidity or just uncertainty about how to proceed has been a characteristic of my attempts at starting these relationships, as demonstrated by the next couple of examples.

I had known a certain girl since I was very young; she used to live next door to us until we were both about seven years old, then our ways parted for quite a number of years, but since her father and mine were both in the same profession, our paths crossed again when we were teenagers. As families then we would meet quite often, since we weren't far apart, and so after a series of non-happenings characterised by Meaningful Looks and Unspoken Suggestions I wrote her a letter out of the blue explaining how I felt. Even this took a fair amount of courage, and I had no clear idea of what the consequences would be. Fortunately for me it was fairly successful; that is, she made it clear she was quite keen as well. Both families were once on holiday together; one evening everyone else had gone to bed and we both ended up alone in the same room. Briefly, if I had been more certain of myself, I'm sure I would have got what every teenage boy wants. But anyway, in the end I think we were completely incompatible from the point of view of interests and generally not having much in common.

You might think I would have been encouraged by this partial 'success' but once again I was too timid to tell a fellow student at university more or less the same thing, despite having had what was, with the benefit of hindsight, plenty of encouragement, such as getting frequent visits, having her hanging on to my arm (pretending to need to hold herself up!) and generally being decidedly friendly. But once again I felt we would have been completely incompatible, mostly due to my lack of ability to deal with the kind of life she would have wanted. I would never have gone to any of the students' social events which happened quite often around the university and hall of residence, which I think would soon have led to a complete breakdown of any closer relationship.

If there is a point to this, I would say that it is possible to worry too much about doing the right thing. Perhaps this amounts to nothing more than the frequent exhortation to 'Just be yourself'. This is a terrible platitude, but I think that any way of reducing the extreme self-consciousness and low self-confidence, which seems to affect most people with ASD, may bring significant benefits. I have written elsewhere that I often feel like there is someone watching over my shoulder all the time, ready to criticise everything I do, and I'm sure now that to have been relieved of that from the outset would have been nothing less than miraculous. I have no explanation, however, for why I managed to free myself from it *almost* totally on a couple of occasions.

Naturally, one of those occasions was with the woman to whom I am now married. We were following the same university course, and she had always been slightly different from the rest of our group in that she was a mature student and several years older than everyone else. More important, I always had a more comfortable feeling in her company than with anyone else, because she always seemed ready to accept just about anyone at face value and had a knack of getting the best out of people.

I felt quite early on in our relationship that this was someone I could get on with quite easily and who was able to give me at least the time to listen to me. Indeed it was quite flattering to me that she found me a useful source of help with our university course, even though I always felt that she was too ready to underestimate her own ability, so I thought it was quite important that someone should encourage her to feel that actually she was able to do just about everything that was required.

It was probably the fact that we were able to give each other mutual support, although in different areas, which caused our relationship to move quite quickly from one of friendship and help with the university course to one in which we were able to share just about any personal thoughts and feelings. At the time I felt I had a lot of things that needed saying, such as how I felt about how my life had been up to that time, how I felt about my school days, how I felt I was coping (or not) with university life and the greater demands that a degree of independence placed on me, and the need to cope with a more unstructured social environment.

I can't really emphasise enough that to feel totally comfortable in someone's company was almost a completely new experience for me, as well as being extremely gratifying in that Gisela appeared, at least, not to find me totally unengaging.

One or two friends have said that the sexual part of any new relationship tends to be, to put it plainly, rather frequent at first, and this was exactly our experience. However, it was never my expectation that that would always be a defining characteristic of our life together. I have written elsewhere in this book what I hoped to get out of any relationship, and to emphasise the point, I think that simply to be there for each other in good as well as not-so-good times represents the best of any relationship. I am perhaps vaguely aware that I might have taken more out than I have put in, at least on a day-to-day basis, but it has always been my hope and expectation that I would be able to give and receive support as either of us needs it, as well as being able to enjoy things together. Of course, this needs to be understood alongside the problems which I have with a wide range of social events, which are described in other chapters.

The decision to live together under one roof was not particularly difficult. To an extent, we had already done it during our university finals, when Gisela almost took up residence in my room in our student hall (in contravention of several rules)! While it's also fair to say that practical considerations had some part in it, I would never have considered such a move if I had not felt that we could make a success of it. (I have already given details of relationships I have not pursued because I knew they would not have worked.)

I had very few doubts at the time that I was doing the right thing, and even the questions over setting up home with someone else and her children seemed to present few difficulties at that time. We did actually have at least a good working relationship at that time, but it was naïve of me not to have understood that children of primary school age eventually become teenagers with all the difficulties they bring! Naturally, I found the prospect of having to be responsible not only for myself but also for keeping a whole ready-made family fed, clothed and housed was quite daunting, but in the beginning I had no inkling of the employment problems which would appear later. I suppose also that I had some kind of expectation that, since I was making the effort to go out to work, then everyone else at home should make at least a token effort to contribute some kind of help. In the end, however, I have realised that that is not a valid reason for someone in my position to have children at all (this is not the Third World, after all; we do not need children to help us to subsist).

It's also worth making clear that, at first, and although it remained unspoken, I was quite sure that I never wanted to have any children. This was for both selfish (the expense, the loss of freedom) and sentimental reasons (not wanting to bring children into a world which I often felt was on the verge of its own self-destruction), and we were mainly careful to ensure that children never happened. However, despite the fact that we were obviously not always mindful of our precautions, I have absolutely no regret that we did have a child of our own.

I would also like to make it clear that (despite what I have heard about a couple of other husbands with AS) I have never considered the possibility of an extra-marital relationship.

I would like to repeat what was said to me by a professional working in the field of autism, namely that people with AS 'do not get married'. So the question arises as to what I hoped to get out of marriage and how I find married life at present. I have already described my attempts at starting relationships, which I felt were never likely to be successful. No doubt this was one of the typical symptoms of AS, in that every last detail has to be perfect in order for me to proceed with something. In any case, during my teenage years, I felt most of the time that my prospects of finding a partner were very bleak, because there wasn't one person out there who would be able to cope with me, and with whom I would be able to cope. I have already said that this person would have to be able to put up with someone who doesn't care for going out much to noisy social events, doesn't talk much but just prefers to 'be with' someone without any specific agenda. Thus, from my side, I wanted someone who wouldn't make demands of me that I would be unable to meet. But beyond this, I was also certain that this person should be at least my intellectual equal, and be able to hold her own in most situations.

The fact is that I got more than this: as well as intellectual ability I got a great deal of sense and humanity, and what is probably best described as wisdom. Therefore my married life has fulfilled these expectations, to such an extent, in fact, that I sometimes feel overwhelmed by the realisation of my own shortcomings in such areas, and it is often too easy to leave Gisela to deal with a situation requiring more tact or discretion than I can easily provide. But I think I could not have found anyone better for me personally. The question might arise as to what we actually do together, given that our social spectrum is quite limited; although this no doubt affects Gisela more than me, for myself, I still enjoy the companionship, the fact that someone is there just to talk to about things that might have happened during the day, about something that strikes me as interesting, and someone to enjoy our free time and holidays together.

There are of course some bumps along the road. I have to admit that I may not always be very willing to live up to the responsibilities of family life, and my desire for my own way of doing things and for more peace and quiet than it's realistic to expect in our situation, are the main cause of friction when it arises. While I know internally that other people's rights have to be accommodated as well, it's not always easy when the house is full of people and noise.

I wouldn't say that my general state of mind is always one of profound unhappiness, but I think I feel more than slightly downcast for a majority of the time. It is one of the more frequent problems in my married relationship that I seem to be unable to prevent this spilling over into the way I deal with everyone else – and I'm sure that there can be few things more off-putting than trying to relate to someone surly and uncommunicative.

Speaking for myself, I find there is very little in what Gisela does that is particularly annoying or irritating. That is, except for the fact that she is inherently untidy, whereas I am the complete opposite. She seems able to cope with living in a completely cluttered environment, where anything might be anywhere…small wonder she keeps losing things!

# 4
# How we met

## *Gisela*

I have been asked more than once, and always by a man, what I saw in Chris. My answer has been to ask the questioner what he saw in his wife. This is usually a good enough answer.

Yet, twelve years down the line, for any couple the vicissitudes of life can make it difficult to recall the heady days of early passion. I do think that Chris is good looking, and I do still fancy him, but what is it about him that makes men question why a woman should be interested in him?

Meeting another man with AS recently reminded me of what I found so attractive about Chris; it was the gentleness of his manner and voice, the hint, possibly, of hidden depths to be discovered. But certainly, there is no suggestion of the macho 'he-man' that many non-AS men believe women desire. In fact, it is the individuality, the lack of a need to conform to some male 'norm' that is one of the AS man's strengths. Chris does not seem to understand prejudice, let alone show it; to discriminate on the grounds of gender, race, disability or sexual preferences would be an illogical, and moral, anathema to Chris. To show disgust at someone's perceived (by Chris) untidy or raucous behaviour, however, is perfectly justifiable to him, even if it does cause uproar.

Chris and I met at Manchester University. We were both on the same course, Russian Studies. This was a small course with only about fifteen students each year, so we tended to stick together. I was certainly not looking for a relationship at the time, and even more certainly not with someone nine and a half years younger than myself.

Chris already had O-level Russian, but I was doing the language from scratch. It was not long before the group realised that Chris was very good at Russian. I marked him out as a possible for helping with 'homework' when I became stuck, which I was sure would happen – unlike Chris, I am not a natural linguist. I remember that after the lesson in which Chris first shone, I approached him and congratulated him on his accent and relative fluency – relative to my painful syllable by syllable torturing of this beautiful language. Chris seemed startled but very pleased that he had been noticed. In fact, it was due to Chris's lack of belief in himself that he did this extra first year; he had been asked if he would like to go straight into the first year of the degree rather than the ab initio course that was a necessity for anyone who had not achieved A-level standard already. Though Chris had done Russian only to O-level, his knowledge of the language was excellent and he could easily have coped with going straight into the degree course proper, but I suspect that his confidence in his academic ability had been shaken by his year at Oxford University, which he did not complete successfully.

Chris loves languages, and it seems a sad paradox that someone with a communication disorder should have been blessed with this talent. It is not only that he has a good memory for words and a fascination for language structure, but he has a very good ear for pronunciation too. He is the ideal linguist. Later on in the course, we

had a party and the rest of the group were bemoaning the difficulties of poetry, and the tedium of lectures. Chris, by this point, had
had a fair amount to drink, but despite that, sat in the middle of the
floor and was able to recite a poem (in the original Russian) perfectly. Everyone was stunned and I was impressed.

In lectures, Chris rarely spoke, but when he did, what he said
was always worthwhile, yet his contributions were so hesitant that
sometimes the lecturer would hold the class to ensure that Chris
managed to get out what he was saying.

Chris was living in a house with five other students; they
seemed to get on reasonably well, and I assumed that he mixed
more with them than with the Russian students, who numbered
only fifteen. Chris enjoyed being part of a group but always seemed
to sit tentatively, both literally and metaphorically, on the edge,
facing slightly away from the group. I suspect that had he been
doing a subject in which the numbers had been much larger, it
would have been more difficult for him to integrate at all.

Because we were a small and disparate group, with a higher than
usual number of mature students and a fair share of oddballs, Chris
did not seem that unusual, although, subsequently, one of our lec-
turers did describe him as unorthodox. As our trip to the Soviet
Union grew closer, so did the group, and we increasingly tended to
share coffee and lunch times.

One day, a lecture was cancelled and I and another girl walked
to the lift with Chris and invited ourselves back to his house for
lunch. He declined to offer us an invitation on that day, but made it
clear that we would be very welcome the following week. On the
appointed day he drove us back to his house and we shared a pizza.

Chris's room was very neat, his desk very organised and he had a
pretty tablecloth over a bedside cabinet on which stood his tea set.
It was quite unlike the rest of the house, which was far more typical
of student accommodation. In the kitchen there were unwashed

dishes in the sink and on the draining area; the rubbish bin was overflowing and the table uncleared. The beds in the other rooms were unmade, the floors barely visible and clothes and towels strewn everywhere. I was curious and rather awe inspired by Chris's more ordered room. His housemates proved to be lovely people, sharing his love of classical music, which had been the factor that had drawn them together and which set them slightly aside from the majority of the other students.

Chris, I, and another friend started to go around together and Chris was wonderful at explaining things to me. He also had a phenomenal general knowledge and I found this fascinating. He would tell me things about the weather, painting, music and a myriad of other things; I enjoyed both his company and that of the students with whom he shared the house. There were some eccentricities, and, generally, I found these amusing. Chris is taller than me and consequently his natural walking pace is much brisker than mine. As he was quiet we would often walk in silence, and I used to drop back and hide to see how far ahead he would be before he noticed that he was alone. It was often two or three hundred yards but eventually he began to realise earlier and earlier that I had dropped back. I found this amusing, but was far less amused when I was going home, and after I had requested that he come with me to the bus stop, he would walk me there and leave me. I suggested that he should wait with me until the bus arrived, and he seemed surprised, but did start to do that apparently willingly.

There was something endearing about Chris: he appeared very shy and awkward, yet he appeared to have a quiet confidence about his ability at languages. He did not have the normal macho anxieties of so many twenty-two year olds and he revealed that a gay friend had on one occasion made overtures to him, thinking that he too might be gay. I could understand how someone might mistakenly think that, yet there is no ambiguity at all about his sexuality.

So, somehow we ended up going out together. I think that I probably made the first move but Chris was quick to seize the opportunity. His housemates said that his mood improved as a result; previously, his brooding depression had affected the atmosphere in the house. Although Chris too says that he had been very depressed at the thought of not having a partner, in retrospect, I wonder whether it was his AS rather than his depression that affected the atmosphere. However, he did have friends or he would not have been in the position of having a house to share. We are still in touch with his housemates through my efforts rather than his, though he certainly enjoys seeing them.

As a result of our relationship Chris became more a part of the group. One of the mature students commented that he had never known anyone as quiet as Chris, but I suppose I did not see it as I tended to initiate the conversation.

In the final year of the course, we both chose the same specialist subject, Comparative Slavonic Philology. We were the only two people doing it. For me, I had enjoyed the History of the Russian Language course, that was the obvious lead into Comparative Philology, but the main attraction was that I could drop Soviet Literature. However, Chris loved the subject and would sit reading the library textbook that was in pristine condition because no one else was interested in it at all.

Whilst in Minsk, in the former Soviet Union, I came across an old book (in English) about choosing a mate, which counselled against marrying anyone who did not like people. At the time, I was slightly concerned about this because I knew that Chris did not always see the best in people and unfortunately people did not always see the best in him either. But, in any case, by that time I felt so involved that I chose to disregard the advice in the book. Apart from the physical attraction, Chris had provided support in a situation in which I had previously always felt alone. I have temporal lobe epilepsy and one of the more unpleasant aspects of an attack is the feeling of fear that overwhelms me. This fear is actually part of the attack and there is little I can do about it. One evening, Chris saw me having a fit and came over and held me; the physical contact was incredibly reassuring. I took this to mean that he must be very sensitive and understanding. I had always felt excruciatingly embarrassed about having a fit in front of someone and yet this was never the case with Chris. It is difficult to explain why this was so, perhaps it was because he did not press for much information; any questions he did ask were factual, and asked without any hint of embarrassment on his part. More important, there was no hint of unease on his part when he was present during a fit.

I must have done most of the talking, but gradually I found out more and more about Chris through persistent, yet gentle, questioning. He rarely revealed anything personal without being asked; there was an apparent reluctance on his part to disclose much about himself, and he explained this away by saying that when he was sent away to boarding school, he had been unhappy and it was this he thought may have led to his inability to express his feelings.

My only involvement with and knowledge of autism was limited to the Kanner type, so there was no way that it would have occurred to me that there was any explanation other than personality or experience for Chris's behaviour. In addition, Chris had suggested that he believed as much himself. A few of us had been discussing marriage and sharing a house. Chris said that he worried about not having any privacy when he was married, and explained that at school he had very little privacy, either in space or of his belongings.

I am sure that I missed many of Chris's eccentricities because I did not have time to notice them: I was too busy being a mother and full-time student, and in any case, when you are seeing someone, the possibility of their being autistic does not naturally occur to you.

I was a bit disconcerted when Chris explained that the only thing he was concerned about when considering moving in with me was my 'housekeeping'. He was not referring to financial matters but to my lack of ability as a housewife. Having said that, he assured me that he would be very conscientious about the gardening, which has not proved to be the case at all!

Despite these reservations, and worries about whether my children would like him, he seemed very willing to move in together, which we did twelve years ago.

# 5

# Diagnosis

## *Chris*

When I read the description of Temple Grandin, which Gisela writes about in Chapter 7, I was still not fully convinced that I was one of these people. However, I have absolutely no doubt at all that my diagnosis is correct. I hope to explain what happened to change my mind, how I felt about the prospect of an 'official' diagnosis, and what happened after it.

For a long time I had been sure that I was slowly but definitely getting better and more socially capable. I don't have any real evidence that this was true but it was definitely the way I felt. Perhaps it was because of the increasing availability of alcohol as I got older! (As an aside, I have often found that alcohol, in moderation of course, helps to loosen a few social inhibitions, although I think in excess it just makes me loudmouthed and uninteresting. And no, I'm not an alcoholic.)

Now that I can look back, not only with hindsight again, but also over a distance of several years, it seems remarkable that I felt both that I had improving prospects and that I managed to forget about how things seemed to start going especially wrong after I left school. In fact, it's clear now that I was certainly not typical when I was at school, but my contemporaries and the school itself, while there were some very big faults, deserve at least some credit for accepting or at least putting up with an eccentric in their midst. The faults were mainly as one would expect, such as not understanding why such an apparently intelligent child had so little to say in class, why he appeared so unhappy and unfriendly most of the time; from my own point of view the regimented timetable, which left little time to pursue my own agenda, and the lack of my own space were big problems. (If anyone thinks that going away to a boarding school teaches you to organise yourself, I can assure them that the opposite is the case: the timetable occupies twenty-four hours of every day and leaves so little to personal choice that all you need to organise are the right books for a lesson.) As for my 'eccentricity', this is either the right or the wrong word, depending on one's point of view. Living in a closed community where not just the school day is shared but also every moment outside school hours, the pressure to conform to 'normality' can be quite strong, and I suppose that anyone not conforming would be seen as eccentric. However, in a fairly large school community there are always going to be a minority of people who are interested in things beyond the norm. So whether that constitutes 'eccentric' or just different is a matter of opinion.

   Despite feeling that my prospects were likely to improve, things started to go wrong after I left school. I went through a period, which I remember lasted in particular between my leaving school and starting university, when I seemed to annoy the rest of my family, irritate them and just generally rub them up the wrong way. With the benefit of hindsight I can tell I was often short-tempered and impatient, and, most important, I couldn't understand why. I sometimes asked myself out loud why I behaved the way I did, and why I felt unable to do anything about it. It seemed to me to be my essential nature. Our family mealtimes were often spent in complete silence and I often seemed to be in the habit of saying exactly the right thing to annoy someone. I wanted mostly not to have to sit with anyone else to eat or generally to interact at all and I found these times particularly irritating. Perhaps in the end I had just become more accustomed to living apart from the rest of the family, especially since (despite what I have written earlier) being away at school became at least tolerable in the last couple of years, with more privacy and space.

It took me perhaps the majority of my time at secondary school (between the ages of eleven and eighteen) to come to terms with the situation. Most of the time I lived at the school except for holidays and occasional weekends. On leaving school my personal situation changed altogether; I was living with people I had spent most of my past eight years apart from. Then when I started university things changed again.

My first attempt at university (Oxford) lasted only two terms. It's still difficult to explain or even for me to understand what went wrong. Academically I felt I had little idea of what I was doing there and in particular what I was supposed to be aiming at in my first year, and how to reach that objective. While I was at school and going through the process of choosing a higher education career, it always seemed to be assumed (not least by me) that Oxford or Cambridge were the right places for me, and I was never encouraged to think differently. I now feel that I should have chosen a course at London University, where the people were welcoming, didn't rest on their laurels and seemed to have a clearly structured idea of the course content. Socially, on the one hand, I had quite a good time, given that at a university I was always certain to meet people who shared common interests with me, if not a common disability. But on the other hand I was hugely frustrated by my inability to form any kind of relationship that was more than superficial. The main problem for me at Oxford was, I believe, the fact that I was never given any clear instructions about what books I should have been reading, what lectures I should have been attending, the objectives to be achieved for each term and so on. I think this must be a symptom that seems to be increasingly recognised to be a characteristic of AS, namely that self-organisation is weak to non-existent, and so instructions, objectives and the means to achieve them need to be clearly set out from the beginning.

Eventually I failed my first set of examinations and I had to leave. Fortunately, several other universities looked favourably on my qualifications from school and I managed to find a place somewhere else. When I started at my new university I was living in university accommodation, but it took me nearly three months before I managed to speak to anyone else living in the same block as me. I think this was perhaps a social low point in my life. I was in a new university, where I had a place more or less as a measure born out of desperation, having had to leave my first university, and I was most uncertain that this was the right thing to do. I had been clutching at straws, attempting to salvage an academic career, and I had managed to hold on to this straw. Worst of all, here was yet another set of new people, and to be blunt, they were much more like the students one might expect to find at any university beyond the ivory towers of Oxbridge. So I was out of my depth immediately.

Despite all these factors, it had never occurred to me that anyone could consider that I was anywhere on the autistic spectrum. I had always thought that autistic people were almost completely incapable of interacting with the real world at all except inasmuch as they used it to fulfil their own needs. I saw the film *Rain Man* and I formed the opinion that maybe autistic people were like normal people only 'more so', in that everyone likes to keep to their usual routine and doesn't like having it disrupted, and everyone is always at least slightly wary about relating to strangers and so on.

So, although I did in fact feel that I shared a couple of these traits, I was a long way removed from the reality of an autistic person.

Gisela describes in Chapter 7 how we found the motivation to get a professional diagnosis, so I won't repeat it here. It is sufficient to say that when we both read about Temple Grandin, it was a revelation. Here was a person who, despite her disability (of which there was no doubt) had made a successful career for herself. Oliver Sacks's book *An Anthropologist on Mars* also contains descriptions of other people with an autistic spectrum disorder. It was only a short time after reading this book that I started trying to find more information about Asperger Syndrome on the Internet. My own approach to sorting through the mass of information was to concentrate on the scientific aspects, which naturally had at their centre the two perhaps most important tools in diagnosing Asperger Syndrome, i.e. the ICD-10 Diagnostic Criteria of the World Health Organisation (see Chapter 6) and the DSM-IV criteria of the American Psychiatric Association. (There are also other sets of diagnostic criteria in use.) It's common for people to look at medical texts about diseases and their effects and to decide that they are definitely suffering from every illness under the sun, so I was very careful about applying these criteria to myself, and of course I did it together with Gisela.

I felt that, as far as our relationship was concerned, the effect of this discovery would be positive, as it would give us a basis on which to make a properly guided attempt to live a meaningful life together, so I had no hesitation about going to the specialist we had found, neither was it any surprise that he had, as he put it, 'No doubt in [his] mind' that I was on the autistic spectrum. I think we were both relieved as we made our way home from the visit.

It became clear from things that Gisela was saying (e.g. 'I don't really want to know about it') that she didn't want to hear any more about autism and Asperger Syndrome again. It was clear that she didn't feel that this was a positive development, which made me a little disappointed, because it meant to me that we would be stuck at this point for ever.

Although I have already said that, with hindsight, I am convinced that the diagnosis was correct, at the time I was still disappointed that there was no prospect of my getting any better. I have always believed that you have to accept things that can't be changed, but in this case, I realised that without a lot of help and effort nothing would ever be better for me. That realisation seemed to become more and more overwhelming, to the point that I think it preoccupied me for a lot of the time. I'm sure that because of this I became even more grumpy and short-tempered, and one day after I blew up over some trivial incident, I had what could only be described as some kind of minor breakdown.

It was at this point that I think we both knew that Something Had To Be Done. Immediately Gisela wrote to the doctor who diagnosed me. He got in touch with my general practitioner (GP), with a recommendation for a prescription for an antidepressant medication.

Unfortunately, since the diagnosis, the general trend seems to have been for me to appear to be even more profoundly affected by AS. This may be due to my using it as an excuse not to participate in any, or very few, social activities, although that isn't the way I see it; the prospect and the reality of dealing with the usual kind of unstructured social occasions have become harder than ever. This of course is no fun for either of us, and I have to confess to being unwilling to make an effort to overcome this. Maybe now that I have more choice over what I will or won't participate in, it is easiest to take the path of least resistance. Another possibility is that the range of interactions necessarily becomes wider in adult life, and so the likely amount of stress this causes is raised in proportion. (This seems even more likely, given the unsettling experiences I have had with employment over the last few years). The responsibilities imposed by being both married and a parent and by the need to earn a reliable income all mean that I don't have the option of retreating from the world to recover for a while, nor can I enjoy thirteen weeks' holiday a year, which I had as a student.

There seems to be little prospect of this situation changing in the foreseeable future. If there is any accessible provision for counselling and support for couples in our situation, then we have yet to find it. Nevertheless, there is growing awareness in the general medical community and amongst the public, so things may improve.

6

# ICD-10 Criteria for Asperger Syndrome

This chapter lists the World Health Organisation ICD-10 (1993) diagnostic criteria for Asperger Syndrome. We have pointed out where and how we feel that Chris meets these criteria, or not.

> There is no clinically significant general delay in spoken or receptive language nor any clinically significant general delay in language or cognitive development. Diagnosis requires that single words should have developed by two years of age or earlier and that communicative phrases be used by three years of age or earlier. Self-help skills, adaptive behaviour and curiosity about the environment during the first three years should be at a level consistent with normal intellectual development.

**Chris:** Apparently this is correct for me.

**Gisela:** Certainly this is supported by what I know of Chris's childhood. He spoke well and clearly, though very little. His interest in the environment had some unfortunate consequences, including setting fire to the back garden.

However, motor milestones may be somewhat delayed and motor clumsiness is usual (although not a necessary feature). Isolated special skills, often related to abnormal preoccupations, are common, but are not required for diagnosis.

**Chris:** I don't think I have any 'Isolated special skills'. I'm not aware that I was particularly clumsy at an early age, although now I may be more clumsy than average.

**Gisela:** Chris has a real facility for languages. He learns and retains vocabulary with ease. As a child he loved maps, and would look at them for hours. He knew and still does know the London Underground by heart. It is difficult for me to say whether or not his preoccupations are abnormal, or just 'nerdish', though I find apparently listening to the background noise on his amateur radio rather strange.

Qualitative abnormalities in reciprocal social interaction are manifest in at least two of the following areas:

- Failure adequately to use eye-to-eye gaze, facial expression, body posture and gesture to regulate social interaction.

**Chris:** This definitely describes me (just ask Gisela)!

**Gisela:** It was the reference to eye-to-eye contact and facial expression that I found particularly striking when I first read these criteria. I had often found Chris's facial expression very difficult to read and had probably irritated him by constantly asking if he was all right. His expression was usually cross or worried even if circumstances suggested that he should be feeling at least content if not happy. I found his awkwardness endearing, yet it seemed that this was actually a feature of a syndrome that had caused him a great deal of heartache.

- Failure to develop (in a manner appropriate to mental age, and despite ample opportunities) peer relationships that involve a mutual sharing of interests, activities and emotions.

**Chris:** I have never been completely without friends, although we have always shared the same kinds of interests.

**Gisela:** I think my definition of friends differs from Chris's. Chris has acquaintances, but he has not yet maintained a friendship on a regular basis. There are people who Chris has known who undoubtedly like him and are prepared to enjoy his company, but in general, I am responsible for our social life and arranging meetings with friends.

- Rarely seeking and using other people for comfort and affection at times of stress or distress and/or offering comfort and affection to others when they are showing distress or unhappiness.

**Chris:** The first part of this is only partly true, but the second part is definitely true.

**Gisela:** Chris will look to me for help with practical problems or difficulties, but I would not describe it as looking for comfort or affection, more reassurance – wanting someone familiar with him. As explained elsewhere in the book, Chris seems to find it difficult to recognise distress and seems unclear on how to offer help or support.

- Lack of shared enjoyment in terms of vicarious pleasure in other people's happiness and/or a spontaneous seeking to share their own enjoyment through joint involvement with others.

**Chris:** Not really true of me.

**Gisela:** My initial thought was that I disagreed with Chris, but I do think that he derives some pleasure from my happiness, though he does not always express it. It is very difficult to know for certain, as often I am unsure as to how interested he is in hearing about something that I have done. I think that is because he is difficult to read, though there are times that he seems more interested than others. I do know there are certain activities in which he likes to ensure my enjoyment!

- A lack of socio-emotional reciprocity as shown by an impaired or deviant response to other people's emotions; and/or lack of modulation of behaviour according to social context, and/or a weak integration of social, emotional and communicative behaviours.

**Chris:** This is difficult for me to tell for myself, although apparently it is generally true.

**Gisela:** I think that 'impaired' best describes Chris's level of socio-emotional reciprocity. However, in some ways I think the main factor that prevents a more empathetic response is an inability to read distress in other people. When Chris sees something that is very obviously upsetting on the television, such as starving children in famine areas, or he hears of someone who has suffered very inhumane treatment, Chris shows a very appropriate response; he has tears in his eyes and also expresses anger at the injustice. He certainly does show a weak integration of social, emotional and communicative behaviours.

- The individual exhibits an unusually intense, circumscribed interest or restricted, repetitive and stereotyped patterns of behaviour, interests and activities manifest in at least one of the following areas:

- An encompassing preoccupation with stereotyped and restricted patterns of interest that are abnormal in content or focus: or one or more interests that are abnormal in their intensity and circumscribed nature though not in the content or focus.

**Chris:** It's true that my interests are quite intense, but I myself wouldn't describe them as stereotyped or restricted. As well as the technical interests, I'm interested in music and art, and mountain walking.

**Gisela:** I am rather surprised by the mountain walking, because I am unable to recall the last time that Chris walked up, or down, a mountain, though he certainly likes high places to test out the reception on his radio. He will sit in front of the computer, or take it apart and put it together (in fact there are currently five in the house, excluding my laptop) for hours at a time. Chris also likes music, but has the tendency to play the same compact disc (CD) over and over again. I bought a CD of horn music, which Chris uses on his laptop, in the car, at full blast on the music system when he is hoovering, and my son and I have now considered doing it permanent damage.

- Apparently compulsive adherence to specific, non-functional routines or rituals.

**Chris:** I certainly have my own ways of doing things and arranging objects, but to me they seem logical and reasoned.

**Gisela:** He certainly does have his own way of doing things, but they do not always seem logical and reasoned to me. All the dishes in the dishwasher have to be arranged in the same way, and if they have not been arranged 'properly', then Chris sets about doing it with such determination that our mugs have a very short life. Items like mobile phones have to be stood up on end, even on the edge of a shelf. To me, logically there seems to be more chance of them being knocked off in that position.

- Stereotyped and repetitive motor mannerisms that involve either hand/finger flapping or twisting, or complex whole body movements.

**Chris:** I'm not aware that this is true of me to any great extent.

**Gisela:** Chris is not aware of this, though I am, and so was the second specialist who saw him. If he is uncomfortable, for example speaking to someone new, even if it is on the telephone, he will twist his ring, or fiddle in a similar way with anything to hand, including a ring on my finger.

- Preoccupation with part-objects or non-functional elements of play materials (such as their colour, the feel of their surface, or the noise/vibration that they generate).

**Chris:**   The same applies here. I'm not aware of it.

**Gisela:**   He loves, and always has loved, to fiddle with knobs, particularly if there is an audible effect from doing so. For example, when he has the stereo on, then he will turn the amplifier switch one way and another quickly.

The disorder is not attributable to the other varieties of pervasive developmental disorder: simple schizophrenia, schizo-typal disorder, obsessive-compulsive disorder [OCD], anankastic personality disorder, reactive and disinhibited attachment disorders of childhood.

**Chris:**   Definitely no history of schizophrenia. Curiously, when I read about anankastic personality disorder, it made me realise how subtle are the distinctions between the possible diagnoses, although I still think that my diagnosis is correct. The distinction between OCD and AS may simply be a question of the other factors that are part of AS, whereas OCD is characterised by obsession and compulsion alone.

**Gisela:**   There has been no professional suggestion that any of these other disorders are applicable to Chris. We have included it because this section is part of ICD-10, and also to ensure that people who may feel that they or their partner have Asperger Syndrome are aware of the fact that there may be other possible diagnoses.

# 7

# Diagnosis

## *Gisela*

In 1997 my brother-in-law gave me a book for Christmas, *An Anthropologist on Mars* by Oliver Sacks.

In his book, Sacks describes seven cases of neurological disability. I read the first six with interest and then arrived at the seventh about Temple Grandin, an American university lecturer who happens to have an autistic spectrum disorder. Sacks writes of Temple: 'She suspects that her own father, who was remote, pedantic, and socially inept, had Asperger's.' I suddenly understood what a bolt from the blue meant. This was my husband and, in fact, Chris had always described himself as socially handicapped. He had been remarkably close to the truth.

The previous summer, we had come very near to separating permanently, for reasons that in no small part arose from Asperger Syndrome. One of the things that I found very difficult was that Chris always seemed to be in a bad mood, he tended to mutter things under his breath and if I asked him what he had said, he would speak much more loudly than I felt necessary and which made him sound as if he were angry. I was astonished at one point when he described me as hostile, because that was how he seemed to me, but he was equally surprised when I suggested that.

A temporary separation was precipitated by an incident at Chris's parents. I had been aware that relations between him and the rest of the family were strained. He would say nothing whenever we went to visit and it was particularly noticeable when the family gathered together that Chris would disappear for much of the time. Finally, Chris had gone up to his parents' house to borrow a tool of some description and arrived to find that his younger brother and his girlfriend were there for supper. Chris had always felt in his brother's shadow and I suspect that he was unhappy that we hadn't been invited, even though we often saw and still do see his parents when his brother isn't there. He walked straight through the house, collected what he had gone for and returned home to say that his brother had been there. I had a feeling that his behaviour would have appeared very rude, but he was genuinely unaware that he could have given out any negative messages at all, because, in his eyes, he had not said anything, so he could not possibly have offended anyone.

In fact, the situation was disastrous. His mother was extremely upset and told me that Chris was no longer welcome at their house. I was caught in the middle, and the only person to ask about how I felt was my brother-in-law's girlfriend. We went some way to sorting the situation out, but it was too much for me because we saw a lot of Chris's family: Linda, my mother-in-law, would pick up George, our son, from the childminder. Suddenly, I was in the awful situation of feeling responsible for ensuring George's contact with his grandparents and living with Chris when I had been embarrassed by his behaviour, and at the same time believing, but not understanding why, he felt that he had done nothing wrong. This was at a time where we had been going through a rough patch. I was working full time as well and it all became too much. Chris moved out for a few days. Despite the fact that living with him had made me unhappy, I was convinced that his intentions were generally good, though I am unable to recall why I was so certain of this.

Until my brother-in-law's gift, the thought of Chris being on the autistic spectrum had never entered my head. I had only a limited knowledge and experience of autism. My first contact with it had been through a friend whose daughter had classic autism. I knew of, but did not understand, the immense practical and emotional difficulties that this had brought the family. Then a few years ago, Chris and I had watched a television documentary about a little boy with Asperger Syndrome. His father was shown leafing through a photograph album of radio masts and the commentary suggested that some parents, particularly fathers, of children on the autistic spectrum showed autistic traits. At the time I laughed as we have gone miles out of our way on a journey if Chris knows that there is a radio mast in the vicinity. Amateur radio remains one of his enduring interests.

I told Chris about the Temple Grandin chapter; after reading it he searched the Internet for more information and found some material including an article that gave the DSM-IV criteria for Asperger Syndrome. I read the article believing that it would show that Chris could not have Asperger Syndrome. He was, after all, thirty-one years old, and even if he were like Temple Grandin's father, it was unlikely that he could be autistic, as things like that 'only happen to other people'. In any case, I still had in mind the little boy on the television programme replaying time and time again the same piece of cartoon video. In retrospect, perhaps I should have remembered Chris's tendency to play the same piece of music again and again.

However, the diagnostic criteria were mesmerising; it was a character portrait, including some physical characteristics, of Chris.

Apart from the obvious criteria relating to social skills I also recognised the poor facial expression and lack of voice prosody.

The ICD-10 criteria (published by the World Health Organisation, in 1993) can be found in Chapter 6 together with comments by both Chris and myself.

We decided that there was enough to suggest that we should pursue a diagnosis. The National Autistic Society helpline was very helpful and provided the names of specialists we could contact privately. For us, unlike many parents, obtaining a diagnosis was the easy part. I was not yet convinced that Chris had Asperger Syndrome. There was the possibility that his painful shyness and 'crabbiness' was a result of his unhappiness in the early days of his time at boarding school.

I contacted the specialist recommended at the Charing Cross and Westminster Hospital and arranged an appointment for 12th February 1997, which was then about five weeks away. I had the feeling when I spoke to the specialist that he might have been a little sceptical. The intervening period was difficult. For me, whatever the outcome, the future did not look bright in terms of a successful and happy marriage. Either Chris had Asperger Syndrome, in which case there would never be that intuitive understanding that one hopes for in marriage, or he was bad tempered and uncaring. I was unable to believe the latter as I had always felt that Chris did care, yet time and time again he did things that suggested the opposite, that he went out of his way to disturb and unnerve people. On the other hand, it was still impossible to believe that he could have autism.

Two weeks before we were due to see the specialist, I received a call at work from a hospital near where Chris worked, saying that he had had a car accident, the car was a mess and Chris was in the X-ray Department as he had a 'bit of low back pain'. When I arrived Chris was flat on his back with his neck in a brace. The first thing he told me was that he desperately needed to go to the lavatory. Despite the fact that his need was very urgent, he had been unable to bring himself to mention it to a nurse, and I couldn't understand why he found it so difficult to ask for a bottle. Eventually, the doctor arrived with the X-ray film, which showed that Chris had cracked a lumbar vertebra. When the doctor asked Chris to sit up, it was clear that he was in severe pain, he almost fainted, yet he had not asked for any pain relief. I recalled the literature that I had recently read which talked about the difficulties people with AS have in asking for help.

It was impossible to put the issue of the possibility of autism to the back of my mind, though it seemed that we might have to postpone the appointment because of Chris's back. However, he seemed as anxious as I was to know one way or another if he had AS. So when 12 February arrived, he took some painkillers and we set off for the hospital. I wondered what the specialist would say; I was most worried that he would say it was a borderline case, or that he could not be sure. Chris told the specialist that he was worried that, having read about AS a little, it may influence his answers. He was reassured that this would be taken into account; subsequently I have learnt that it is the way that adults with AS answer questions that is almost as significant as the answer itself in arriving at a diagnosis.

I can remember parts of the diagnostic procedure: Chris was asked what book he was reading at the time and replied that it was a non-fiction text about code breaking at Bletchley Park. People with Asperger Syndrome are far more likely to read non-fiction than fiction. Some of his answers were a surprise. What would he worry about if he found me in the kitchen having cut myself very badly? Chris replied that it would be whether he would do things right, not whether *I* would be all right. He was also asked where he would put himself on a scale of nought to ten, where nought was someone who needed complete order and routine and liked nothing to be different, and ten was the opposite. This was our incompatibility put on a numerical scale; Chris said he would like to say two, but he felt the answer was one, and I know that I am an eight or nine.

At the end of the procedure, the specialist said that there was no doubt in his mind that Chris was on the autistic spectrum and had Asperger Syndrome. It was not a shock as I thought it would be, because, I suppose, it was the logical explanation for all the difficulties that he (and I) had experienced. The specialist was very pleasant, but what help could he offer? Chris is 'high functioning', apparently independent. He is too able to make use of the few services available to adults with autism, yet the services available to people not on the autistic spectrum in times of need are often not appropriate. I commented to the specialist that we had had difficulties in our marriage and I did not think that the usual marriage guidance would have been constructive, given Chris's difficulties in communication. Whilst I appreciated the specialist's comment to Chris that he should hang on to me because I was understanding, I would like to feel that there was someone to whom we could occasionally turn for support. He also advised me that I would have to be very explicit about my own requirements and when I jokingly suggested flashcards, he countered with 'Try it'.

That evening I picked up a sheet of information that we had received from the National Autistic Society (NAS) and looked at the publications on Asperger Syndrome. I realised that I simply was not interested in autism as a disability. It held no fascination for me, certainly not to the level I was going to have to become involved, though having qualified as a physiotherapist, generally I am interested in disability issues.

Nevertheless, we started off with the excellent NAS publications including *Why Does Chris Do That*. Whilst it provided some answers, there was nothing about marriages in which a partner has Asperger Syndrome. As soon as it arrived, we both devoured Uta Frith's book, *Autism and Asperger Syndrome*. Gradually I became more and more fascinated as the idiosyncrasies of my husband were revealed as part of a pattern that others shared to a greater or lesser degree.

Chris's initial reaction seemed to be one of relief: he was no longer inept, as he had always thought, and it was not his fault that he struggled in social situations. He had always semi-seriously described himself as socially handicapped, and ironically, he had been absolutely correct – everything seemed to fall into place and there was a name for it. However, this relief was short-lived.

The NAS provided the contact name for a partners' group and it was interesting to know that there were other people in our situation. At that time all the people in the group were women who were partners of men with Asperger Syndrome, reflecting the much greater incidence of autistic spectrum disorders in males. Many of the group had struggled for years in a marriage with a partner who had been eccentric, to say the least, and many women had left or wished that they had left the marriage. As the diagnosis had given me some hope that our difficulties could be addressed, I was devastated to find that there was no one who had much to say that was positive about their marriages or their husbands.

What compounds women's feelings of isolation in these marriages is the scepticism of people outside the marriage. 'My husband doesn't understand me' is the cry of many women, and individual signs of the AS can be seen in individuals who are nowhere near the spectrum. I am an extrovert, but I love lists and playing with numbers. So when a close friend suggests that you are making a mountain out of a molehill, while you are aware that your partner really does have a profound disability, it can be very frustrating and heighten the feeling of isolation. In some cases, the partner with AS is reluctant to accept the diagnosis, and there can also be opposition from the partner's family to accepting that the person has a disability. It is far more comfortable to think that a family member is 'different' than that they have a disability.

I have been fortunate. Not only did Chris accept and, initially, welcome the diagnosis, but also we had the full support of his parents, who at last had some explanation for why, despite their best efforts, Chris seemed to be so unsociable and uncommunicative. It explained all the fiddling he had done as a child and his near-death experiences, including setting fire to the back garden and trying to drop a lighted match into a car fuel tank, to see what happened.

My main source of support in this period was Pauline, who lived in the house whose garden backed on to ours. I was given her name by the National Autistic Society. We discovered that we had been corresponding with each other for years because she was an accountant and at that time I was a tax inspector.

Pauline's son had Asperger Syndrome, and Pauline ran a county support group for parents of children with AS. Pauline is totally committed to doing the best for her son, and she knew Asperger Syndrome 'inside out'. She had decided, as far as possible, that she would try to see the world from her son's point of view, because then she would be able to help him deal with it. Her insight was invaluable and started me on constructive lines. As far as I am able, where Chris does something that is not entirely acceptable or socially appropriate, I try to look at it from what I understand to be an autistic viewpoint. Though lacking Job's patience, this has helped me appreciate Chris's strengths as well as the difficulties caused by Asperger Syndrome. This is not looking to Asperger Syndrome as an excuse for 'men behaving badly', but more a way of considering if it is an explanation for something that he has done or not done, said or left unsaid.

One other invaluable piece of advice from Pauline was to read and reread, as often as necessary, the literature on Asperger Syndrome. It is easy to read the material, and understand it, but comprehension of the disability takes much longer and without Pauline's many hours of friendship in the early days after the diagnosis, Chris and I would have foundered. Since then, her husband has been of help too, schooling Chris in job interview techniques.

Although most literature is aimed at parents of younger children with Asperger Syndrome, it requires little imagination to see that many of the issues remain the same throughout the life of a person with Asperger Syndrome. It is easy to see Chris reflected not only in the people described in those books, but also in the many children at all points on the autistic spectrum whom I have now met. The local support group too was a very helpful contact in the early days; if nothing else, here were people who could understand the difficulties I was encountering and who could also understand why I had found Chris attractive in the first place.

I had met children with Asperger Syndrome and was eager to meet other people with Asperger Syndrome, and the opportunity arose to hear Temple Grandin speak at a conference. This would also be the first time Chris was to meet someone in his 'AS family'. A couple of weeks before the conference, both Chris and I and Temple Grandin had appeared on the same TV programme, although Temple's bit had been shot in the United States, and our bit in Britain. When we arrived at the hall where the conference was being held, we went over to speak to her. She was sorting through some slides, and didn't look up at all, though she recalled with interest spending time with the producer of the programme. We agreed that we'd probably meet later. As we came away, Chris observed that she didn't seem to want to talk to us; I think that he was shocked when I explained that that was precisely how he appeared to other people.

At the coffee break, Temple made herself available to discuss problems with people, and of course, she was surrounded by people who wanted their own specific questions answered. Chris stood back, away from the throng watching her, and said simply, 'That's like me'.

We had lunch with Temple (fortunately for us, not many people at the conference wanted to spend their lunch break with her) and she and Chris chatted across the table, without looking at each other, both fiddling frantically with bottle corks. It was at that meeting that I think Chris realised that he would take medication for the rest of his life, and that if it made a difference, then it was worth it. For me, it brought home the fact that I was married to someone with a real disability. I wondered how I had failed to realise that his acute shyness and endearing awkwardness were not what they seemed.

A few months after the diagnosis, Chris became increasingly unhappy, culminating in what was almost a breakdown. He had been rude to friends of my children from my first marriage and I was angry and upset. I shouted (always the wrong thing to do) and Chris shouted back, stormed a bit and then collapsed on the settee in tears. For the first time, he refused to respond to my trying to help and, also for the first time, I turned to his parents for help with our marriage.

Chris's father talked to him and then came through to where Chris's mother and I were sitting; he looked dazed and said 'He thinks totally differently to us'. Although I was aware of this, it became my first real insight not only into the level of mutual comprehension, but also into the complete lack of self-esteem that Chris suffers.

We contacted the specialist who had diagnosed Chris and he recommended our local GP prescribe Citalopram, which Chris has been taking ever since. Sadly the specialist was on the point of retirement but he did suggest the name of another specialist; it was in her that we placed our hope for help with dealing with this disability, which continued to threaten our marriage.

Chris was as eager as I to improve matters. At the hospital we waited for the specialist to arrive, but when she did I immediately sensed scepticism. She questioned Chris and accepted his initial answers. Was he happy at school? 'Yes', he replied. This was news to me: no mention of the bullying; crying at night; taking himself off to the library all Wednesday afternoons to read the *Encyclopaedia Britannica*; leaving a window open in the computer room so that he could go back later to fiddle. For me, this seemed particularly poignant, that a child could lead a life of relative isolation in what was a community, predominantly, of children.

Vainly, the specialist tried to get Chris to talk at length about one of his special interests. Chris just does not do that: he is not a talker; despite being a gifted linguist, he does not know what to say. If you are lucky and allow for processing time, then he will talk. Chris answers questions especially if the question provides a structure for the answer, but he rarely enlarges. I sometimes think that the words 'yes' and 'no' are the words he uses most often and almost always as the only word in a reply to a question.

This specialist questioned the diagnosis. We were staggered, and then in my case offended and saddened, when she said that people with Asperger Syndrome do not marry. As another partner has asked, it seems very odd then that it is considered to be a genetic condition. I asked if that meant that she found people with Asperger Syndrome unattractive. She did not reply. Chris has subsequently been recognised by other professionals as having Asperger Syndrome and I strongly dispute the belief held by some people that men with Asperger Syndrome do not marry. They do, as Chris, many others and I know.

We both have, at various times, been on Internet lists specific to issues related to autistic spectrum disorders, and we have found these both helpful and depressing. Many parents struggle just to get a definitive diagnosis for their children to enable them to have the schooling that is every child's right – and the diagnosis is frequently the start of more battles, for extra help in school, entry to a specialist school and prevention of unnecessary exclusion. Chris received the diagnosis, but there is virtually no other help available, certainly not on the National Health Service (other than medication for anxiety). It is right that priority is given to children, but the lack of help for the autistic adult, who on the face of it is independent, is like denying a hearing aid to someone who has been diagnosed as deaf.

The only support available to Chris is me, and there is no doubt that the diagnosis has enabled us to help our marriage work.

# 8

# Communication

## *Chris*

Scratch the surface of the professional literature about autism and Asperger Syndrome, and you will soon find that communication difficulties of one kind or another play a very central role in the diagnosis. Needless to say, therefore, that communication problems may be just about the most trying difficulty in any Asperger marriage. This is certainly true in our case.

First of all it's worth making the point that interpersonal and written communication are two very different things. Beside myself, I know at least one other person with AS whose spoken communication is characteristic in its lack of variety and range of expression. But when this same person puts pen to paper, or keyboard to email, then you would never be able to tell. This may be a useful thing to remember if you can get your AS partner to sit down with a pen in the first place! I have to confess that making the initial effort to sit down and write, and the prospect of having to put something down on paper, are far harder than the process itself, despite the fact that Gisela has encouraged, prompted, cajoled and bullied me into telling her how I feel in writing, given that I seem to find it so hard to do it face-to-face. So I'll say this for my own benefit as well as for any readers: I know somewhere at the back of my mind that any communication is better than none.

If you're thinking something along the lines of 'Why can't (s)he just talk to me' then you are not alone. Unfortunately this question is never going to be answered, if you ask it in that way. There have been so many occasions when I have just not known how to respond to something. The times when this happens are very diverse, but a couple of examples come to mind immediately.

I work in a very relaxed environment, and I suppose wherever a majority of men meet together there is a certain amount of banter going on more or less continuously. Also people often make mildly jokey comments at each other's expense. This is part of normal human relationships and everyone understands it. For me, however, where most people seem ready with a quick answer, I am often tongue-tied and embarrassed for want of an appropriate response. The best I can do is a weak smile and no more. (Although when it comes to word games and puns I can hold my own against anyone!) I think this is probably why people sometimes see me as humour-less.

I've heard people say that they don't like small talk. Nevertheless, after so many years of watching people indulge in it, I'm sure that it's essential to oil the wheels of human interaction. Only in my case not only do I not like it, I feel that I'm completely at a loss for an appropriate subject. Naturally, if I've just come inside from the freezing cold, it would be normal to comment about that fact but there is a whole world of inconsequential conversation which I think I'm missing out on. Strangely though, I don't usually feel the lack of it – inconsequential is just that, and, to my mind, unnecessary. On the other hand, when the occasion calls for it, I do wish I could partake.

I can only speak for myself, but in some situations I often feel that I'm watching myself trying to deal with it, and there is no more critical observer than myself. I don't know whether this counts as ordinary self-consciousness or not, but it is almost impossible to get rid of it. Right now as I type, I feel like I'm looking over my shoulder scrutinising every word. This especially seems to happen when the situation doesn't call for a spontaneous response, for example, in an intimate situation, or when we are arguing about something, which I deal with below. This means that we don't enjoy what I take to be the usual husband–wife chitchat which they use when (they think that, not always correctly) no one else is looking.

I know that Gisela discusses the 'argument problem' in Chapter 9, so I will put my point of view. For years after we started living together, Gisela would get annoyed about something and start haranguing me: it wouldn't really be correct to call these incidents 'arguments' or 'rows' because they were almost entirely one-sided affairs. She would shout and get more and more worked up because I simply didn't respond. This would sometimes lead to the loss of an item or two from the kitchen, as Gisela describes. So what did I feel when this was going on? It would only happen rarely that I felt Gisela didn't have at least some justification for the point she was trying to make, which didn't make it any easier for me; I hope I'm at least reasonably perspicacious in seeing another's point of view. But the need to understand what the other person is feeling is perhaps very important in these situations, and that is precisely an ability which I don't have. I can see the logic or otherwise in an argument or proposition, and I feel as strongly as anyone else about some beliefs I have, but I can only understand someone else's feelings in relation to something I have experienced myself. So emotional appeals are not likely to be very fruitful for anyone whose partner has AS. (I talk about feelings in Chapter 10, so let it suffice here to state that people with AS do have feelings, and they are as individual as everyone else's.)

Also there was the problem of feeling like I was watching myself get more and more into difficulty, which rapidly turns into a spiral of hopelessness and self-reproach. When you are convinced that whatever you are going to say is the wrong thing, it's easier to say nothing. This in turn leads to regret at not being able to make a useful contribution, and so on. I would so often feel physically hurt at some of the things that Gisela would say in the heat of the moment, because I knew that in reality they were not true, but I had an insurmountable difficulty in proving it.

One obvious result of this is a spiralling decline in self-esteem, and the conviction that everyone else knows I'm no good, in particular Gisela herself. Sometimes this reaches the level of mild paranoia, when I think everyone at work is talking about me behind my back, and of course Gisela is only putting up with me rather than getting anything positive at all out of the relationship. I have often thought that this is the reason why I like quiz nights and *University Challenge* so much: it gives me a chance to do something, however pointless, that I'm actually quite successful at.

I recently left one job very suddenly. For several months I had felt that my employer's intentions and the real necessities of my job were quite different, and things never really improved, so we parted company by agreement. (My employer at the time knew nothing about my AS.) I had however managed to keep all this from Gisela, so when it actually came, it was quite a shock for her. This illustrates quite well the difficulty which still exists, I feel, in our relationship, although I think after this lesson I wouldn't make the same mistake again. Gisela was convinced that I should have told her the moment I knew things were going wrong, while I was sure that if I had told her I would have had to deal with an 'ear-bashing' ten times worse than anything I had ever experienced. So somehow I managed to convince myself that I would muddle through. I think this question is still unresolved in my own mind, but I hope I never have to force the issue by telling her again that I am in difficulties at work.

I would also like to make a point about survival in the outside world, and this especially includes work. It's probably fairly obvious that the relationships one has at work are quite different in character from the family relationship. On the one hand, the normal day-to-day stuff of working life is quite formalised even if not always formal, and that is quite easy to deal with. The extra-curricular situations, for example post-team-meeting meals and social occasions also are easier to deal with than the domestic problems I mentioned above. There are certain boundaries which are not crossed on these occasions. As a quick example, ten-pin bowling has been in my experience quite a popular social activity with work colleagues. In any working environment worth working in you will be able to enjoy the activity for what it is and not as an occasion for personal embarrassment. Remember that any decent set of colleagues are not there to see you fail. Also there is sometimes (even sometimes free) alcohol to ease the seized social machinery a little. But despite this there are some social activities organised at work which I would not attend, for example Christmas parties, where it is expected that there will be loud music and dancing.

Nevertheless, I feel that the best I can hope for is to be no more than competent at communicating the necessities and perhaps something more in the family situation. Perhaps this is all that is required to survive the outside world, but it doesn't guarantee a successful personal life without understanding from families and partners.

# 9

# Communication

## *Gisela*

Difficulties with communication lie at the heart of most of the problems we have encountered, both in our own relationship and in Chris's relationships with other people.

It is almost impossible for someone who is unfamiliar with autism to understand the effects that it has on day-to-day communications and the problems that Asperger Syndrome raises in a relationship. On the face of it, we both speak the same language – in fact Chris speaks perfect Standard English using a wide and active vocabulary. So where is the problem?

In some situations Chris communicates extraordinarily well. He is particularly good at explaining things and was a point of reference for many students at university. I have noticed too that he is good now when dealing with employment agencies; essentially, in both these situations there is an unwritten script. In the first, Chris is sharing matter-of-fact information, which he does well as there are few unexpected questions and the answers are all in the 'script of his knowledge'; and in the second, he has learnt a script for the answers that he now knows to expect.

Yet the most extraordinary thing that I have learnt about Chris, whilst we have been writing this book, is that he does not regard the 'intimate' conversations that he has with me as spontaneous. And, of course, these are the conversations that oil the wheels of all successful marriages.

When women say that their husband doesn't talk to them any more, often what they really mean is that their husband refuses to discuss a certain issue with them or possibly does not tell them what they want to hear, or just that the couple are growing apart.

However, in Chris's case, when I say that he doesn't talk in emotive situations (he doesn't say much generally), I am speaking quite literally. He does not say anything, answer any questions, respond in any way at all, except with complete silence. It is difficult to believe this is possible, let alone understand it, unless you have experience of autism. It is useless to try any of the usual feminine tricks to try and persuade him to talk. In fact, it has been so long since I used them I had to ask my sister for examples. Sulking is pointless, the 'You don't love me anymore' tack is also a complete waste of time. Chris just remains completely and utterly silent.

A breakdown in communication is, of course, a threat to any marriage, but in our case it cannot be put right by sheer goodwill and the usual couple counselling. Even before Chris's diagnosis, I had discounted 'Relate' (a charity providing the services of trained couple counsellors) as being of help, as this would involve talking, which is not something that Chris can do easily.

For me then, one of the most frustrating aspects of our marriage has been the impossibility of discussion of any issue that may be at all emotive. Typically, problems would arise when I wanted to raise a point over something that Chris had done, or not done.

The first time this happened was only three months after we had moved in together. Chris was supposed to pick me up in the afternoon from hospital after a minor operation for which I had had a general anaesthetic. He didn't arrive. Not only was I upset, but I grew increasingly embarrased as the nurse kept returning to see if I had at last been picked up. Taking a taxi was not an alternative because the hospital was insistent that I be accompanied on the journey home by a friend or relative.

Eventually, I rang Chris at work, and to my astonishment he was still there, long after I should have been collected. He had been unable to bring himself to explain to his manager that he would like to leave to pick me up and had been hoping to slip out without being noticed. I was very uspet and pretty angry. Surely I was more important then a temporary embarassment. Chris arrived and I hoped for an apology and some concern for how I felt, physically and emotionally, but far from it. *He* seemed cross and I became more and more cross myself. We drove home in silence and Chris remained silent even after we arrived home. I saw to the supper for all of us, which made me even more unhappy and resentful. (There is nothing like self-pity and a sense of injustice to bring out the worst in me!)

Finally, six hours later, after some more 'probing' on my part, he said angrily that there was nothing he could say and he was angry at himself for letting me down. But until then, he had said nothing. His obvious regret was more than enough to make me feel better, and I was just sad that both of us had gone through six hours of misery. He has subsequently said that saying sorry in such a situation is hopelessly inadequate, when, of course, saying nothing is so much worse. And, I know that, for me, a genuine 'sorry' and a gesture of affection goes a very long way.

Chris seems to think that I resurrect this incedent because I am still angry about it, but he is very wrong. I look back at it and remember it as one of those times that he ultimately let me realise how much I mattered to him.

Since then the pattern of disagreement would be that I would raise the issue and naturally expect a comment in return, hoping of course for an apology and an attempt to put things right. But there would be silence. Nothing, not a word, not even a glance of acknowledgement. I would construe his absence of response as irritation or annoyance with me for raising the subject. Like a child who has been ignored, I would press for attention, pushing the original issue, again to be met by silence. Even the most trivial of issues would become blown out of proportion, because the issue would change into Chris's apparent unwillingness to discuss anything or attempt to put it right. I would be almost jumping up and down in frustration, once hurling at him that a wall was more responsive. On demanding that he at least look at me, he would take me literally and do just that, staring at me, but still wordlessly, which certainly did not improve the situation. Occasionally, at night, when pushed too far, Chris would suggest that I would be better off going to sleep! I now understand that this was as much a practical suggestion made out of concern for my welfare (and his) as well as a vain attempt to end a situation that he was struggling to deal with.

Though I am not violent, this total passivity was so frustrating that I would go into the kitchen, choose something relatively worthless and throw it at the floor, and then have to tidy it up. This was never anything that I had ever wanted to do in the past, or only very rarely. I found myself weeping with anger and frustration, and then realising that it was pointless. Until we had the diagnosis, and I became aware of how differently Chris thought, I assumed that his response (complete lack of response) was deliberate and possibly designed to wind me up. Immediately after the diagnosis, I decided that there had to be a better way of dealing with my frustration and for some time, if a similar situation arose, I would try to calm down by playing 'Patience' on the computer or doing some sort of puzzle, nothing that demanded great concentration. However, this meant staying awake very late on a regular basis, and this would anger me more.

Time and time again, I explained that he should either apologise or disagree with me, at least say something, yet he never seemed to do that. Finally, one day, some time after he had been diagnosed, I asked Chris why he did not say anything, and eventually (there is a long processing time) he explained that he simply did not know what to say.

A further complication was that often Chris was silently feeling that he had 'failed' yet again, but because he did not say anything, I did not know that that was the case. This was particularly sad, because that does suggest that he genuinely regretted what he may have done or not done and that was all I wanted to know. My continued nagging must have compounded his feelings of 'getting it wrong' and eventually causing his anger with me. Because he does not understand what I am thinking then he could not resolve the situation by saying something to mollify me. Understanding why he is silent has helped a great deal, but it can still feel frustrating.

I do try to explain that I have needs, and that they have not been met; for example, I was doing some painting and, in the absence of any practical help from Chris, I would have liked some acknowledgement of my results but it was not forthcoming. (Though nowadays, this is less of an issue, because I would be clear about what help I wanted.) However, there are times, when for my own good, and if I am really angry, that it is essential to get over to Chris that the issue is so important to me that I have not been able to remain calm. This has frequently been to do with Hugh, Henry and Olivia. I am concerned that if I seem to be dealing with a situation and say simply that I am unhappy, he will not be able to differentiate between a fit of pique and major emotional upset.

Silence can be a tool in itself for communication; it can be used to anger someone, yet in Chris's case, I have no doubt that his silence is not intended to have any effect on me at all. I believe that he is silent for no other reason than an inability to communicate appropriately in an emotionally charged situation. I have seen no evidence that he has the social 'intelligence' to be able to manipulate someone else's mood by refusing to talk to them.

I have realised too, that when faced with obvious anger, Chris withdraws into silence through fear of saying the wrong thing. I have learned the value of remaining calm and rational, and this has benefited all other areas of my life. However, although remaining calm and rational can be beneficial, in sorting matters out, to stay like that when you are feeling very emotional feels unnatural and quite stressful. I want to shout what I am really feeling, or 'have a go' knowing that anything said in the heat of the moment will be seen as that. Though this can be damaging in any relationship, the effects in ours are worse and much more difficult to mend. Each word I say to Chris, even those I really don't mean that are hurled in anger and frustration and designed to hurt at that moment because *I* am feeling hurt, is heard and mulled over and, worse still, remembered and accepted as genuine criticism; even those words that are said kindly can be misinterpreted.

Yet subtlety just doesn't work. Sometimes I have wanted to say something that could be construed as critical, and in couching it in gentler terms, Chris does not understand what I am saying. So I may try to put it another way. Recently I have discovered how to tell when Chris is confused about what I am trying to say. He will repeat the last few words of the sentence that I have just said, or make some comment that appears pedantic, when in fact what he is doing is trying to pick through, what seems to him, I suppose, a jumble of words to arrive at the precise meaning of what has been said.

I also tend to make the mistake of discussing more than one issue at a time, which is not helpful, and I am aware that he is trying to listen and at the same time trying to understand which issue is which, whether the issues are connected, and which issue is the most important.

Giving instructions can be difficult too. It is necessary to be explicit. 'You must ring me if you are going to be late home, because I will be making supper, and in any case you should think of me, and I have to pick up George, I work too you know' loses Chris completely. Even 'You must ring me if you are late' has proved to be inadequate. What is far more successful is 'If you do not catch your usual train, you must ring me up, as soon as you can, to tell me that you have not caught it'. I have to be specific both about on what occasion he should make the phone call and at what time the call should be made.

It can take Chris a long time, minutes sometimes, to reply to a question, particularly if he senses that there is an emotional edge to it. Generally, I only notice this when I am wanting to discuss something personal, and I have to fight against an irritation at the length of time he takes to answer, sometimes three or four minutes. I have discovered that I can move things along if I go to leave the room. However, this irritates him because he senses (quite rightly) that he is under pressure to make a reply. As someone who enjoys communicating, I find it almost impossible to imagine how it must feel to be put in a situation where I am unable to say what I want to say, and also to have the doubts, as Chris does, about what should be said in the particular circumstances.

Occasionally, things do go wrong. Having explained carefully, calmly and rationally why I feel upset, I will check that Chris has understood, and when he replies 'Not really', there is the old temptation to find something expendable in the kitchen. Most men would have had the sense to say that of course they understand how

I feel, even if it is only to prevent any further hassle. Generally, though, the diagnosis provides an explanation for his reaction and also has helped me deal with these situations more constructively. Rather than pressing an issue, I walk away and try to put the particular problem in perspective. Though Chris does not usually apologise, it is clear by his actions that he has acknowledged what has been said. His apology may be by way of a cup of tea in bed, or a packet of liquorice Catherine wheels – a great delicacy for me. The trouble is that most women want issues sorted out there and then, yet, apart from the fact that I want immediate reparation, there is no good reason why a genuine non-verbal apology cannot be made later. It is *me* that has the problem here, and ideally we need to find some sort of compromise. What makes matters worse, for me, is the impossibility of following the age-old advice to 'never go to sleep on an argument', because Chris seems to go to sleep to escape resolving those issues that he finds difficult to deal with. The only thing that prevents him from sleeping is indigestion. In the early days, after one of these unresolved arguments, I would be stalking around the house becoming more cross, while Chris would be upstairs sleeping like a baby. Chris's ability to fall asleep in any position, in almost any situation is quite remarkable and a friend has suggested that it is rather like a screen saver, which seems to me to be a perfect analogy.

Maxine Aston in her book *The Other Half of Asperger Syndrome* suggests turning the lights off or down when preparing to talk with a partner with Asperger Syndrome, and this has helped a number of people I know in similar relationships. In our case though, it is a disaster as the dark makes it easier for Chris to go to sleep, and I cannot even see his eyelids drooping as a warning. I ask a question, leave a reasonable length of time for a reply, and then I am much more likely to be rewarded with the sound of regular breathing than a considered response.

## Scripts

With my first three children I tended to adopt what a friend described as 'morals rather than manners' approach to guiding them (I am uncomfortable with the connotations of the word discipline in raising children). That is to say, I expected them to take into account the feelings of others in their behaviour, so, when they had been to someone's house, they should say thank you to the person they had visited, not because it was good manners, but because it showed appreciation for the efforts that had been made by their host. They were expected to behave in the classroom because the teacher had a difficult job looking after thirty plus children etc. On the whole, this approach worked fairly well with my older children.

However, there is a flaw in this approach when dealing with the person or child with AS, because their mind-reading skills make consideration for someone's feelings more difficult. For them, a script and directions for use are far more effective and less ambiguous.

I have noticed with Chris that he does pick up phrases and store them away for use in the future. The phrases may come from something he has heard on a television programme to something that I have said.

I was made particularly aware of this when he agreed to help me out manning the bran tub at the Christmas Fayre at our son's school. A row of children waited patiently for their turn to pay twenty pence to find some knick-knack out of the bran tub filled with paper shreddings. I would make comments like 'Go on, dig deep'. Chris at first said nothing at all. After a while he began to speak to the children too, and I realised that he was using exactly the same phrases as myself with precisely the same intonation.

I am certain that scripts are one of the ways that would enable Chris to deal more effectively with some of the situations that arise socially and with us, but advice on this would be far better from a professional, rather than myself.

## *Non-verbal communication*

Speech is such an apparently complex skill and a major and obvious milestone for young children that the much more subtle, but equally important acquistion of non-verbal skills tends to go unnoticed. Indeed, in my husband's case, there was a failure to notice until the age of thirty-one, and yet it was the recognition that these were absent when I saw the diagnostic criteria that most strongly suggested to me that a diagnosis of Asperger Syndrome was a possiblity.

## *Facial expression*

Misunderstandings arise over non-verbal communication, principally facial expression. I had not realised how essential non-verbal communication was: I had heard of body language etc., but equally important are those little smiles that people do without even thinking, such as the ones that mean 'Hi' or acknowledge the presence of another person. The absence of those generally speaks volumes, but in Chris's case, it can mean nothing. The problem is trying to gauge whether or not the lack of a smile is disapproval, irritation, annoyance or not of significance. For example, if someone enters a room that is already occupied, they will, at the very least, glance at the person who is already there. Generally there will be a smile and usually a word of greeting. All of these are missing with Chris. He is as likely to walk wordlessly and unsmiling into a room and turn off, or on, the television or the stereo without reference to anyone already in the room. There is no intention to annoy; he is simply reacting to his own needs. I am used to this and it causes at the most irritation, but to other people, unfortunately, it appears very ill mannered. This is compounded by the fact, that if the person is a stranger, Chris is anxious and even less likely to make any kind of communicative gesture at all.

His facial expression, as with many people with Asperger Syndrome, is fairly flat, which I have, in the past, interpreted as being cross. I no longer continually ask if he is all right, as in the past he used to become irritated with my regular questioning. A friend, who had not met Chris before, told me recently that, had she been unaware of his Asperger Syndrome, when she delivered a package to the door on one occasion, she would have thought him rather rude. Again, Chris certainly had no such intention; he seems to be anxious about unexpected interactions with people he does not know.

However, just as Chris is unable to alter his Asperger behaviour, I cannot prevent my 'normal' non-Asperger person's instinctive response to somebody who, through an absence of the appropriate 'friendly' signals, appears hostile. There are still times where I react inappropriately and become irritated; other people in the family also have problems with this. Often it feels that there is an aura of gloom and unpleasantness around him, which is totally uninten-tional, and this is magnified if he is unhappy about something that someone else has done. For example if someone has not washed up their dirty dishes, rather than asking them to do it, he mutters some-thing under his breath that no one can hear, and refuses to repeat it, which is infuriating because nothing is resolved.

He also tries to communicate displeasure in other ways that are equally unconstructive. If one of the boys left something in the bathroom, perhaps on the sink rather than tidily on the window sill, Chris would toss it back into their bedroom. By doing this he had perhaps satisfied his own irritation, but done absolutely nothing to ensure a harmonious atmosphere in the house. This has been the cause of a lot of my unhappiness.

But non-verbal communication is more than facial expression and body language. Chris also lacks those nods of the head and 'mms' that are used by the listener in a conversation to express interest in what is being said. I wasn't aware of non-verbal communication until Chris's diagnosis when I discovered that he had a lack of it. Yet this is a vital part of social communication and a lack of it is very detrimental to fluent and successful social interaction.

A measure of Chris's difficulty in reading non-verbal communication himself was revealed by his attempts at British Sign Language (BSL). It had surprised me that although he is an excellent linguist he had not been very successful with the BSL classes that we had attended together. Unlike me, he was very good at remembering signs and found the language structure fascinating, but unusually he was unable to understand the signing. After the diagnosis, I realised that the problem was the facial expressions that are an important part of the language that had beaten him.

## Tone of voice

Tone of voice is another, very vital, part of the communication process which can alter the meaning of the actual words spoken. Before the diagnosis, Chris returned from an interview and commented that though he had felt he had answered well, he thought that he had sounded monotonous. I am not sure that this was the case, but certainly he does sometimes use an inappropriate tone that can, unintentionally, suggest irony. He may make a positive comment, but the flatness of his voice makes me wonder if he is being sarcastic. However, after considering the context, it usually becomes clear that it is more than likely that the comment was genuine. On the other hand, Chris may make a comment that he intends to be humorous, but his voice belies that, and I take the comment seriously and feel upset by it.

One of the most striking examples of an unfortunate use of tone is when Chris is offering sympathy. For example, I might say that I feel unwell, or something has gone wrong. In the early days, he would make no comment at all, which was unnerving and rather upsetting; then from somewhere, Chris picked up the phrase, 'I'm sorry to hear that'. This is a much more appropriate reaction. However, it is said in a bright and cheerful tone, which is not really in fitting with the meaning of the words. In fact, knowing about the diagnosis has enabled me to be happy that the sentiment is genuine, even if it is not completely apparent.

## Volume of voice

Chris has what I describe as 'poor volume control'. He speaks very quietly, particularly if he is depressed, and it is fair to describe it as muttering. If I ask him to repeat what he has said, the volume shoots up to loud, and unfortunately this suggests impatience to me. That probably is not the case, but it is difficult to prevent an instinctive reaction to a feature of communication that would, in the majority of people, carry a certain meaning.

## Conversation and small talk

Conversation with Chris is very different from conversation with someone who is not on the autistic spectrum. Tony Attwood suggests that partnerships like ours can be compared to relationships in which each partner is of a different culture. It is sometimes helpful to think of two languages, 'Asperger Syndrome' and 'non-Asperger Syndrome' and allow for a few misunderstandings in both directions. It is particularly essential to stop and think both about what I have said, and about Chris's response. This lack of fluency makes conversation seem very difficult.

This was brought home to me when Chris worked in the United States for a couple of months. After he had been away for four weeks, I went to San Francisco to see him, and he was delighted and clearly moved when he picked me up at the airport. I was too tired that evening to talk and it was not until we went out for a meal the next evening that I realised how difficult it can be to have a conversation with him. Chris has a tendency to one-word answers to questions, and this can kill conversations, because the fluidity of a conversation between two people is dependent on similar levels of input from both contributors. It is quite easy for a conversation with Chris to degenerate into what feels like an inquisition.

**Gisela**: Did you have a good day at work?

**Chris**: No.

**Gisela**: Were you busy?

**Chris**: Yes.

**Gisela**: Did anything interesting happen?

**Chris**: No.

**Gisela**: Any problems?

**Chris**: No.

So many of these exchanges between people who are familiar with each other are not really about the words that are being spoken, but more a way of saying 'I am interested in you'. And this is where Chris finds small talk difficult, because he is not aware of its real meaning. There is the additional complication of all words having meaning with Chris. He says few words, but those that he does say are important. He tends to speak in full sentences, even if they are only one word long, whereas most people ramble and the people to whom they are talking pick up the gist of the conversation. Chris lacks the ability to infer, so if you don't say precisely what you mean there is the capacity for misinterpretation, and Chris is able to quote you back verbatim to prove that you did say what you didn't mean! So, while he has an extremely good understanding of irony in a literary context, where it is expected, in a day-to-day conversation, he may take an ironic comment literally.

As a footnote to the time in San Francisco with Chris, I should say that we had a lovely few days together. He drove me back to the airport, and said to me that if I didn't mind, he would rather not come into the airport with me. I know from experience that this was because he was sad that I was leaving. For me that was more than good enough. Love expressed slightly differently from the traditional way of simply saying 'I love you' is often far more touching and convincing.

Some time ago, we called at Chris's parents' house; his mother asked if he had had a good day at work, and he replied 'Yes'. This gives finality to the exchange: the single word suggests that the speaker does not want to continue the conversation, rather than they do not know how to continue. I tried to explain afterwards that she was showing an interest in him, and he should acknowledge that by saying a little more than 'No' or 'Yes'. Chris asked for an example of a fuller reply, and I suggested that he could say something along the lines of 'The traffic on the M25 was busy today'. Chris looked bemused and replied 'But it is always busy'. This brought home to me the complexities of social intercourse, especially small talk, where we say something, yet the meaning is unrelated to what we say. And the absence of these pleasantries can speak volumes, but in Chris's case, it is wrong to assume that the absence has any significance at all.

Chris rarely initiates conversation, and after a period of time with a good communicator, I do notice this, and feel regretful that this is lacking. It is not that he is reluctant to tell me things (usually) but there seems to be less of the urge to share experiences, than for other people.

Even after living with Chris for twelve years, I still find it easy to misinterpret his one-word responses as being unsociable. I do speak in a different way to Chris from the way in which I speak with other people, and it is hard work, possibly comparable with speaking in a foreign language.

People with autism understand the literal meaning of language, so an autistic child hearing the expression 'raining cats and dogs' will think that cats and dogs are falling from the sky. Chris's reaction to language is inclined to be literal, so a question, 'Do you want a tea or a coffee?' will be answered as 'Yes'. The non-autistic person would understand from the context in which the question had been asked, that the real meaning of the question was 'Which would you prefer, a tea or a coffee?' Again, it is easy to interpret the unhelpful answer as being deliberately obscure, when that is not the case at all. It can often be Chris's humour, he enjoys the concept that there are two meanings, one literal and one implied, in much of everyday speech, though I suspect that the literal response is always the first that comes to his mind.

### Eye contact

Another difficulty is Chris's lack of eye contact. This is not generally a problem now, as he usually seems quite comfortable looking me in the eye. However, eye contact is phenomenally important in successful communication. In addition, I had always thought that people with autism were not able to do more than one thing at a time, yet Chris is quite convinced that he can read and listen to me at the same time. I am unconvinced. So I now say, 'Please close the newspaper and look at me so that I know you are listening'. I can see the logical comment that of course Chris has offered, which is that he does not have to look at me to listen, but I need him to. This can mean moving the paper so that he is not checking the headlines and practising his skill of reading at a distance of four feet.

I am aware that to some people I must sound condescending, yet it is simply trying to deal with what, in many ways, is as much a disability of communication as hearing loss.

## Literally speaking

Chris loves word play and one of his favourite television programmes is *Third Rock from the Sun*, in which four aliens adopt the form of human beings and come to earth to study humankind. Much of the humour derives from the aliens taking the language literally and this appeals to Chris, as does the following joke, which we first heard at a conference on autism.

> A helicopter was flying around above Seattle when an electrical malfunction disabled all of the aircraft's electronic navigation and communications. In the clouds and haze, the pilot could not determine the helicopter's position and course to steer to the airport.
>
> The pilot saw a tall building, flew toward it, circled, drew a handwritten sign, and held it in the helicopter's window. The pilot's sign said 'WHERE AM I?' in large letters.
>
> People in the tall building quickly responded to the aircraft, drew a large sign, and held it in a building window. Their sign said 'YOU ARE IN A HELICOPTER.'
>
> The pilot smiled, waved, looked at his map, determined the course to steer to Seattle airport, and landed safely.
>
> After they were on the ground, the co-pilot asked the pilot how the 'YOU ARE IN A HELICOPTER' sign helped determine their position.
>
> The pilot responded: 'I knew that had to be the Microsoft building because they gave me a technically correct, but completely useless answer.'

Chris said at the time that he would have given precisely that answer. Occasionally these literal replies can be infuriating, but usually they are engaging and one of the real advantages of living with someone with Asperger Syndrome.

They can cause difficulties, however, and are one of the causes of Chris's echolalia that I find so frustrating when we are trying to talk. I was extremely angry about something that he had done, and I concede that I was over-reacting as one of the three children from my first marriage was involved. I described his action as 'way off-line'. This was a major issue for me, and it was infuriating to have it reduced to a repetition of 'way off-line' as though I had used a phrase that was incorrect. But of course, what was really happening was that Chris was trying to work out what on earth I meant, using a computer or technological term in a conversation that was on a subject very far removed from technology.

*Turn-taking*

Turn-taking is a critically important skill, and it is easy to recognise the person who doesn't know how to do it and interrupts when people are talking. But it is not that simple. Fluent turn-taking in an informal conversation (the type that Chris experiences most difficulty with) involves occasionally latching on to someone else's turn, interrupting slightly and providing the encouraging noises and smiles of feedback referred to earlier. A large proportion of the time, turn-taking is done correctly, but everyone occasionally slips up and feels a little embarrassed because they have got it slightly wrong. For the non spectrum person, though 'getting it wrong' generally means speaking out of turn, but for Chris, the problem is that he seems unaware of the necessity of responding to a statement unless it is a question. Yet a failure to acknowledge a statement can seem like a deliberate attempt to sabotage a conversation.

For example, non spectrum people would automatically make some response to the following statements:

> It's a nice day today.

> I have had a bad day at work today.

> I really think you owe me an apology.

> You look tired.

But they are not questions, and so Chris is very unlikely to respond.

In addition, turn-taking involves a regular exchange of conversation. With Chris, this is not the case and he can take several minutes to reply. This can make conversation very laboured and so discourages people from continuing.

The most difficult thing about Asperger Syndrome, from my perspective, is that it is always easy to mistake autistic behaviour from such an able person as being deliberately unsociable or manipulative, when almost invariably it is not. I can understand why people not on the spectrum find this inability to communicate so difficult to understand. Chris's hearing is excellent; he has a very good musical ear and is multilingual. He can get by in a number of European countries, and speaks mostly German with my (German) mother; he has provided specialist computer support in English, French, German and a bit of Russian. He can get by in Dutch and Spanish and has more than a smattering of Italian. Yet, he finds it painfully difficult to understand other people in a setting where there is a lot of background noise, and cups his hand around his ear to try to help concentrate on the one voice. He finds it hard to follow more than one conversation at a time, though his command of the English language is apparently perfect, to the point where he cannot help correcting others.

With Asperger Syndrome, to anyone unfamiliar with autism, there is usually no identifiable sign of a disability. I have sometimes wondered If it would make life easier for Chris if he wore a visible hearing aid, except people would shout at him and he can't stand that, as I have discovered when he puts his hands over his ears if I talk too loudly because it is physically uncomfortable for him.

As life goes on, this communication does not get any easier. I know that it is as difficult for Chris as it is for me. Yet, for me, those difficulties contrast very starkly with the ease of communication with other people in my life, family, work colleagues and friends. While Chris's main weakness is social communication, it is my strength, and I think that this is where many of the difficulties arise in marriages like ours.

It makes sense that relationships like ours start to succeed where the person with Asperger Syndrome meets someone who is a good communicator. The person with Asperger Syndrome makes the effort to communicate; however, making the effort all the time is fine when one is courting or not under pressure, but when communication becomes an essential rather than a nicety, for example, to sort out misunderstandings, or provide sympathy, then this is where relationships can suffer.

For me a major frustration lies in embarking on a 'discussion' hoping that this time something will be agree or achieved, and again hitting a brick wall. I have very rarely had an emotionally charged exchange that has left me feeling satisfied or happier in any way or feeling that anything has been resolved. Yet I cannot say that this is Chris's fault; it is simply one of the difficulties cause by Asperger Syndrome.

Successful communication is very significantly affected by external factors, so if I am under pressure at work, not only do I need some intuitive understanding, but also I am less able or even willing to make the additional effort required to keep the lines of communication open. In addition, if Chris is under pressure, he is likely to withdraw to the computer, saying even less than usual. I am sure that this holds true for most marriages, but much more so when one of the partners has Asperger Syndrome.

We have found email is useful, to the point where we will email each other even though we are in the house together. Email allows Chris to say how he feels as he has more time to collect his thoughts and express them without any external pressure. However, I have still found it of limited use in sorting out areas of disagreement: Chris also has the ability to push away unpleasant issues, and it is very easy to ignore emails that you do not want to answer.

Very recently Chris has introduced me to the 'instant message' facilities on the Internet. This has allowed us to have some fruitful and, from Chris, some very witty exchanges. I have really enjoyed these, and though Chris may be 25 miles away, I can feel closer to him than when he is in the same room. Chris can of course log out if he doesn't want to continue the conversation, but the evidence so far is that he will not do this, and more important, we have been able to discuss issues that have in the past proved to be impossible to talk about face-to-face. It may be the physical distance between us which means that all he has to deal with in the exchange is the words I have written, totally uncomplicated by any non-verbal communication that can be more complex for him to understand – such as anger or irritation. Also, on messenger I write in sentences and stick more to the point so that this too helps minimise any ambiguity about what I am saying. The fact that there is time to think between exchanges without any pressure to respond is helpful to Chris as well. It seems to be easier for him to express himself too and there is less possiblity of being misunderstood because the tome of his voice does not match his words. Finally, the messenger services seem more successful for us than email, perhaps because of the immediacy, Chris knows that I am still at the keyboard and 'speaking' to him and so is less likely to delay or fail to reply.

## 10

# Affection, sentimentality and intimacy

## Chris

Gisela invented the title for this section. I would have chosen something different. I detest sentimentality, which I think is a wilful display of empty emotion over matters of no consequence, and it really should be avoided because it devalues the true expression of feeling.

How do the majority of men feel about their partners? I suppose that in reality one would get a different answer for each time the question is asked, but I'm sure that, discounting those relationships where break-up is inevitable, there must be some common thread, and I think that I share that thread.

Sometimes people seem designed specifically to get on other people's nerves, and that goes for husbands and wives as much as anyone else, perhaps differently in character, but it happens nevertheless. But the defining quality of the relationship which I share with Gisela is that, despite the things which irritate me about her, and which I know are never going to change, these are insignificant details on the broad canvas of my feelings towards her. Although I have written about Gisela elsewhere in relation to her particular abilities, it would not be much of a relationship were it to be based on nothing more than what she can do for me materially. To say that I am emotionally attached would be understating the matter: attached with thick steel cables might be more appropriate. I can state quite honestly that, when I have nothing else demanding my full attention, scarcely an hour goes by that I don't think about her in some way.

And, strangely, if I were able to wave a magic wand and change her essential nature, the way she manages to make an empty room untidy, or her apparently chaotic manner of moving towards some purpose (although she always gets there in the end), then I would be living with a different person altogether, and in truth I would not change anything.

It needs to be made clear that I enjoy (or suffer?) the full range of emotions. Indeed, I think that sometimes some of my emotions are excessively strong: unreasoned, blind prejudice makes me spittingly angry; children who suffer at the hands of their parents, the same, and I have sometimes felt I have come close to causing a public scene over what I would describe as parental abuse of children. However, there are certain emotions which seem to get blocked somewhere on the path between evocation and expression. In our situation as a married couple, were my wife not so intelligent and understanding, I think there would have been serious difficulties at a very early stage (and in fact there have been difficulties, although it has not yet come to the point of separation). I have an enormous difficulty with the verbal expression of affection. It is not just a case of feeling embarrassed or self-conscious with it. I understand that this may be difficult for anyone else to understand, but it takes a great effort of will to tell my wife how I feel about her. She has frequently encouraged me to write things down, which I regret I have not made very much effort to do, but this is a method that may prove quite fruitful.

On the other hand, there has never been a problem with the physical expression of affection, given the time and the opportunity. We both seem to lead such busy lives that it's just about all we can manage to do to keep work and home running on an even keel without even thinking about making time for other things! Also I have to admit that I am mostly uncertain about the right moment for making a physical approach, which further reduces the amount of opportunity. But when it does happen it's usually pretty successful. Of course in the absence of verbal expressions of affection, this side of our relationship is quite important, so needless to say, more opportunities would be most welcome.

It's difficult to pick out individual things that make me feel particularly affectionate. I think that in fact I feel that way most of the time, in the absence of anything which has made me a bit annoyed or irritated. Something as small as a look or a smile, however, can make a whole day seem brighter.

Partners are supposed to 'care for' their other half, and again I find it difficult to describe any individual actions that I would describe as specifically designed to express caring. Perhaps on a purely practical level, when Gisela is particularly busy (never let anyone say that teachers have an easy workload!) then I tend to take over things like cooking in the evening, and with a few other household duties like washing the laundry and so on; but I'm sure there are many other things I could do besides. Regrettably, as well as the verbal difficulties I have described, I have a big problem remembering important dates, which creates another problem when I should remember to get a birthday or wedding anniversary card. So the overall picture, at least as far as appearing to be caring, is that I could do much better than I am at the moment.

# Intimacy, romance and intuition

## *Gisela*

When I first met Chris, he appeared to be very shy and was very sensitive to touch, though I think much of this was an autistic fear of people, and a natural shyness as much as true tactile sensitivity. However, I did notice that if he were touched whilst he was asleep, then he would start in his sleep. The response was very marked though it has lessened since he began medication to deal with anxiety. Surprisingly, then, there were and never have been any problems with the 'physical side' of our marriage, although I understand that this is not always the case for people with Asperger Syndrome.

However, there is an effect physically in the normal day-to-day touches of reassurance. Chris is unable to comprehend where a hug would make all the difference, and indeed let him off the hook of communicating verbally. The occasions where he has offered help in this way are rare, and all the more precious because of it. There is no reluctance on his part though to touch; he notices if I am less tactile than usual and it obviously disturbs him, as eventually he will make a comment about my being 'less friendly'.

The obvious answer would be to ask for a hug when I feel the need for one, but it is often when you are most in need of comfort that you feel least inclined to say that you need it. However, over the years, I have learned to explain what I am upset about and say that a hug would help. Chris has, in the past, come up with what he believes is a useful response by providing a helpful suggestion for dealing with whatever I am worried about, for example, he may suggest that I discuss a work concern with a manager. Thinking logically, it does make sense that for the person with AS, a hug is not the obvious answer to a concern about work. Often all I want is for someone to say 'Don't worry', or 'It will be all right' even though you know the problem is still there. The words of reassurance can provide a temporary comfort, yet I can understand that this sort of platitude is just not in the vocabulary of a person with AS.

Intimacy is not purely physical and it is the emotional aspect that is more affected by the AS. A belief commonly held by people in a long-term, successful relationship is that they know what each other is thinking. This is far from the truth in our case and it was not until some time after the diagnosis that I became aware of the extent to which we totally misread each other's thoughts and intentions. It is as difficult for me to 'read' Chris as it is for him to 'read' me. I suspect that misunderstandings occur because each of us imagines the other to be thinking how we might ourselves think in the same situation; yet AS and non-AS perspectives are very different so we are almost bound to be wrong, myself as much as Chris.

I am often surprised that, given Chris does not understand me emotionally much of the time, he seems to think that I know what he is thinking all the time. It is as if he is aware of only one consciousness – his own. This can cause problems. Friday evening is our 'Chinese Takeaway' evening, and we do not order this until Chris arrives home. One Friday evening he did not come home. I waited and waited, but did not hear from him. I had tried to ring him on his mobile, but either he had switched it off, or it needed charging. It was not until well after 10:30 that I heard from him. He had gone out for a drink with some colleagues. I was pleased for him but asked him why he hadn't let me know where he was, and reminded him that he worried if I was out later than I had said. He said that he knew he was all right; when I explained that I had been worried, he sounded surprised and even grateful, asking 'About me?' I am certain that it had not occurred to him that I would worry, and I am not sure whether this was a reflection of his low self-esteem or that he really assumed that as he knew he was safe, then somehow, I did too.

Chris and I have lived together for twelve years now, and it becomes difficult for me to remember how the non-Asperger male behaves. I am sentimental about things that the children have given me, or things that were special to them when they were little. I don't think that Chris understands this at all. When I was decorating one of my sons' room, I thought that I had accidentally thrown out some of these precious items and was very upset. Chris's main concern was that he might have done it and was worried that he would be in trouble; he was totally unable to understand why I was so upset. He shows no attachment to gifts that I or anyone else have given him, but I suppose that there is little beyond the material value in these items in any case. Their value for sentimental reasons lies only in the fact that the gifts are a reminder of the care that someone has shown in their selection for the intended recipient.

A few years ago, Chris worked in California for seven weeks, and I stayed in the UK. We 'spoke' to each other by email, sometimes several times a day. These exchanges were probably some of the most successful we have had and I was saddened to find that Chris had erased them when he was doing something (yet again) with the computer. They mattered to me and though Chris had clearly enjoyed them, they were not as important to him. But of course, he is more likely than I am to remember the contents word for word.

A major obstacle in making amends where things have gone wrong is in Chris's complete lack of understanding how I feel. He may be quick to feel anger at himself for 'getting it wrong again' but he does not seem to appreciate that anger with himself will not put right the emotional hurt that I feel. Worse still, he is simply unable to understand what I feel or why I feel that way. So we are left with a yawning chasm in understanding. When I first realised that this was what was happening, I was at least able to stop the cycle from hurt to anger that I experienced by distracting myself. It took me some time to really understand the profound differences on the way our minds worked. I also have to accept that Chris is never going to know what I am thinking. I am never going to have those 'romantic' moments where he is reading my mind.

Occasionally, if he really wants to make amends, he will disappear in the car and return with a bunch of flowers which he hides, unconvincingly, behind his back and then thrusts at me, with obvious embarrassment. He does not seem to realise how much these gestures are appreciated and remembered.

### Compliments

Chris does not pay compliments particularly often, and these really are another form of small talk. They are immensely difficult for the person with Asperger Syndrome to manage easily. Which compliment do you pay to who, and on what occasion? Telling a strange woman that she has gorgeous legs might get you into trouble, but say it to your wife and the response could be very different. The idea of the 'negative compliment' is also complicated. Your wife has her hair cut and the fact that you have not made a comment suggests that you do not like the hair cut. This must seem nonsensical to the person with Asperger Syndrome. The advantage is that when Chris does say something complimentary to me, then I know that he really means it and it is not simple flattery.

However, the compliments are rare, so I was delighted when Carole Gray gave Chris a copy of her 'Compliments' booklet. This contained a very useful table detailing the frequency that compliments should be given. So you give someone at work, say, one compliment a week, but your wife merits one a day. Excellent. The compliments came on a regular basis, until the booklet was no longer next to the bed to remind Chris. I had been unable to understand why they had suddenly stopped until weeks later I found that the booklet had slipped some way under the bed.

I went through a period at work where I was quite unhappy, and was finding the combination of a difficult manager, four children and my first husband's new wife difficult to handle to the point where I was losing sleep. If I woke Chris up to say I was feeling anxious, he would give me a reassuring hug, and so I was quite astonished when he said some time later that he thought I could cope with everything. I wondered what I would have to do to let him know that things were getting too much. I have realised that his sensitivity to my frame of mind is much greater when there is an effect on him, that is when my behaviour affects him. Typically, after an unresolved argument, I may take a while, usually a day or so, to sort myself out and realise that the issue was not important enough to merit any further thought and Chris's relief that I am back to normal is clear. He seems more relaxed and anxious to do something to keep me that way.

Like many people, when I am tired, I am less predictable. Chris finds it particularly difficult if I behave out of character, and I can see the panic on his face when I blow a fuse over something that may be quite minor. I would like him to understand the underlying cause, that I am tired or particularly anxious, but even if I explain that, he is unlikely to make allowances, presumably because my behaviour has been illogical and therefore unreasonable.

## Romance

Perhaps it is because he has known me for so long that Chris no longer has any problem with eye contact with me, though looking into each other's eyes lovingly is not a part of our lives. Like many men, Chris made more effort in the earlier days of our relationship to give me cards, gifts and even to remember my birthday. One difficulty arises in the differing levels of importance that we each pay to these special days and tokens of affection.

For Chris, celebrating his birthday is not that important, though for a couple of years, his parents were away on his birthday and for some reason he seemed to feel affronted. For me, and my children, we do like the gifts that are part of special days, but it is the writing on the birthday card and the thought that matters. It may be clichéd, but these occasions are an opportunity to say things that should be said at other times, but often are not. I have kept all the cards that the children have given me, including the handmade one from my son, wishing me a 'Happy 29th Birthday'. To Chris, cards seem to hold little importance: he signs them 'love Chris' and puts a row of crosses, almost as though it is a duty to be carried out. It is also possible that Chris is as economical with the spoken word as the written when it comes to this subject.

However, the odd emails that I receive from him during the day somehow convey a greater warmth. Perhaps he feels happier in the more technological medium.

Chris has bought me presents in the past, but it is difficult for him to imagine what I might like. Often he has bought me something such as a classical CD, that he knows that he would like, presumably confident that my taste will be as impeccable as his. He was rather disgusted last year when my 'Christmas list' included 'Beatles' and Classic FM compilations and asked what on earth I wanted them for.

One way of compromising on having a present that is a surprise, but one that I would like, is to guide Chris in a certain direction, but leave Chris to make the final choice. Perfume is a successful example of this type of present.

## Attachment

I am older than Chris and so at a time where many of our mutual friends were on the point of marrying, some of my friends were on the point of splitting up. On hearing of another separation, Chris expressed disapproval and this reflects his attitude to our relationship. I have sometimes suggested to him jokingly that I felt secure that he would not 'stray' because of his difficulties in 'chatting up', but, in truth, it is because I feel I can count on his loyalty.

It would be untrue to say that separation has not crossed either of our minds, but if we could remove all the pressures of everyday life, such as employment and running the house and family, then we would be very happy. I am sure that this goes for many couples, but I do believe that Asperger Syndrome makes life harder for both of us. Yet those times that are often seen as stressful for married couples, such as Christmas and the New Year, are always enjoyable for us. I often think how useful it would be to have the opportunity to think like Chris, just for a few hours to help me appreciate his difficulties.

It is sometimes assumed that because people with AS find it difficult to empathise, they are unsympathetic and uncaring. I have found this to be far from true. It is the perception of someone's distress that is often the issue. Where Chris does recognise distress he does sympathise. The sight of starving people and emaciated children brings tears to his eyes. He is angry when he hears of injustice. When someone is ill he is ready to help, and is always ready with the practical solution: 'Take a tablet'. However, he is unable to make the soothing and sympathetic comments that often are as effective as the medication he has suggested. Why should he? In practical terms, 'TLC' (tender loving care) does very little. Recently though, I have noticed that if he hurts himself, he expects me to show an interest and complains if I do not; this has coincided with his own attempts to verbalise sympathy. I have also learned to be explicit about what I want: a hug, a cup of tea, a hot water bottle or whatever else might help.

I have also become used to not expecting things to be done without asking for them. It is very easy to feel resentful that my needs have not been anticipated, to believe that Chris isn't thinking about me and even to think that his lack of attention is deliberate. However, there is plenty of evidence to suggest that Chris does care and wants to help; he just needs some prompting. More recently, particularly since I started teaching, he has shown consideration without my asking for it.

One of the early indications that a child may have an autistic spectrum disorder is the absence of pointing. That is, there does not seem to be the need for the child to share experiences with others. This is certainly so with Chris, though gradually over the years, he has become more inclined to share things. If something goes wrong, then he is likely to turn to me to help him sort it out, and he does contact me to share a success he may have had, but it is sharing the little day-to-day things that is missing. Occasionally he will tell me something, and once he came galloping down the garden to tell me that he had seen fox cubs in the garden next door. This was exceptional, not only because he wanted to share something he had enjoyed, but also because of his obvious excitement.

The impressions then that I sometimes have is that it doesn't matter whether I am present or not, but that is not the case. He much prefers to do things like going to the cinema, a play or a concert together and in fact will avoid doing these things on his own.

Chris told me once that he loved me. I have since discovered that it is not necessary for the person with AS to repeat these small intimacies that are frequently part of a relationship; the fact has been stated once, and that is enough. For most women, I imagine that the lack of these regular affirmations is disconcerting, and, yes, I would enjoy some more obvious romantic gestures, but Chris is not really able to do this. However, there is enough for me to know that I am important to him, and in any case, I am sure that, contrary to the romantic stories we women like to believe, not all men are the knights in shining armour that we would like them to be. I would still like the occasional touch of romance, the unasked-for little note or gift, to happen more than once every five years or so – but it doesn't happen and so it seems to me to be far more rewarding to look at what is successful about our marriage.

Unlike me, Chris has never said anything to me that he has intended to be malicious or hurtful; he would not do it. And he wants this marriage to work. I have no doubt that marriage for the man with Asperger Syndrome is very stressful, despite the benefits, and Chris does make real attempts (usually) to do what he thinks is right.

The one thing that saddens me is that Chris's inability to express himself has made me feel awkward about telling him how I feel about him, and has even discouraged me from using endearments with him.

## 12

# Sex

It has been suggested that some men with Asperger Syndrome have little interest in sex, and that both men and women with AS experience difficulties in this intimate side of their relationships.

There has been only one research project devoted to couples in which one partner has Asperger Syndrome. Currently it does appear that there is too little information available on the effect of AS on the 'physical' side of marriage. It is not unreasonable to postulate that the communication difficulties with resulting unhappiness and feelings of isolation for the non Asperger Syndrome partner may stand in the way of a successful physical relationship. Sensory issues for the person with AS and other features of the autistic spectrum could also make successful sexual relationships more difficult to achieve.

Of course, it is also easy to forget that in the general population, many couples do not always enjoy a satisfactory sex life.

For us, fortunately, this part of our marriage is very happy, and unlike Homer and Marge Simpson we do not have the urge to make it public, so we are keeping this chapter short and discreet.

**Chris**:    The only thing to affect the frequency of our sex life is the availability of energy and opportunity. Having sex gives me the opportunity to communicate things that otherwise would never be spoken.

I had learned all the mechanical details at school but it doesn't prepare you for the emotional aspect, which, I think, is quite successful in our case.

**Gisela**: Though shy of hand-holding etc. at first, Chris seemed very quickly to enjoy physical contact, and I feel that when we make love, it is done in the literal sense of the word.

The only routine is the comfortable reassuring one of familiarity with each other, and certainly not the fixed routine of the obsessive. But that doesn't mean that we are averse to trying something new!

# 11

# Living together

## *Chris*

The way we organise our domestic responsibilities doesn't follow any routine that we decided from the start, in the sense that we drew up some kind of plan of action. Instead we fell quite early on in our life together into a pattern that has remained mostly unchanged since then. It's worth pointing out that this is an area that has caused a certain amount of tension and probably will continue to do so.

I have always been very keen on making sure that everything in the house has a place and that it should always be in that place when not in use. To me, this seems completely logical, and ensures that when I need something I will always know where to find it. This is becoming especially important now that my previously infallible memory is failing somewhat as I get older! (Well, actually it was never reliable at remembering dates of birthdays and so on, or important messages, but that's another matter.) However, with so many people in one house which was probably never meant to hold as many as it does, there often just seems to be not enough space to keep everything, which is a problem which I only add to by insisting on keeping so many computers at home. This is why I find it especially irritating to find things that aren't 'where they should be', and I can't be happy until everything is put away. What is more, I seem to be the only person who finds this a necessity.

In this respect Gisela is the exact opposite of me, at least that's how it seems to me. I think she has a tendency to leave things where they fall, with the obvious consequence that when she needs to find something it's not clear where it will be. This also means that in order to do any cleaning at home, half of the time is spent just clearing surfaces and spaces so that they can actually be cleaned. Apart from the irritation this causes me, it seems completely unnecessary because I think it's counter-productive not only because the stuff needs to be cleared away, but also because it creates more work when something needs to be cleaned, and more stress when something important goes missing. There are probably very few people who have a similar set of responsibilities to us who can keep track of absolutely everything all the time, and leaving anything and everything scattered in random places helps not a bit.

Looking after the garden is supposed to be my responsibility, and I have to admit, I have been quite negligent of this over the years. At the moment some parts of our garden look more like a jungle, although I always keep the grass cut when I need to. I'm not a fan of all the gardening programmes on television. In fact I prefer to avoid them because they remind me of what I should be doing. The same goes for the rash of DIY (do-it-yourself) programmes that has infected our screens for some time now.

It wasn't my intention to list what I do and what Gisela does in this chapter. The examples above illustrate the different approach that Gisela and I have to domestic responsibilities. Keeping the house clean and tidy and the garden in order are details that form only a fairly small part of all the responsibilities that come as part of owning and running your own home. But for me they loom very large to the exclusion of most other things, while for Gisela, they are not as important as the major responsibilities of keeping the domestic finances in order and making sure that the fabric of the house is intact. In fact if Gisela had not organised our mortgage and dealt with all the legal details of buying the property, then we wouldn't be living where we are now, and in fact we probably wouldn't be living together at all.

Now all this gives the impression that Gisela is negligent of some domestic things, which is far from the case. What I have tried to describe is my immediate feelings about the way things should be, when in reality my activities tend to be restricted to certain areas, so that as long as I'm happy with 'my areas' then everything else tends to be insignificant. So the truth is that Gisela is

The professionals say that while, in general, men are better at dealing with the details of something, women are better at seeing the big picture, and I think in our case this difference is magnified, hence my concentration on wanting everything in its right place before I can even consider anything else, while for Gisela it's important to ensure that the correct framework is in place so that everything can be fitted into it. These two approaches should perhaps complement each other well in the domestic situation. If I am honest I frequently feel that Gisela doesn't pull her weight domestically, but if I ever voice my frustration at this, then she's very quick to make me understand that I am in the wrong, resulting in my feeling guilty for saying it. This easily leads to a vicious circle of resentment and self-recrimination, and it is probably the reason why I sometimes feel I spend half my life apologising, when a moment's thought on my part would have made me realise that the complaint would be completely invalid anyway.

As for financial matters, I just hand over a sum of money every month to Gisela, and out of what I have left I pay some regular bells, for example telephone, gas and so on. That is as far as my involvement goes. This has been characteristic of our relationship from the earliest days. If it weren't for Gisela's ability and willingness to organise the mortgage for and processing of our house, we probably wouldn't be living together at all. So from that time I suppose I have just let matters develop into the way they work now, which is that Gisela deals with anything requiring detailed attention. This of course means I have a relatively easy time given that I rarely apply myself to such matters, and sometimes, in fact probably quite often, Gisela is loaded down with concerns over and above just work and family and I know she feels that she sometimes simply has too much to think about. My excuse is that I have to spend time studying for professional examinations, which is a rather feeble excuse given that I do most of this on the train to and from work!

I suppose that the reality of the situation is that, given the slightest opportunity, I am all too ready to lapse into idleness and to let someone else do all the important things. I don't truly believe that this is due to AS. Regrettably, idleness doesn't make me feel any better, but when I make the effort to do something well, then I feel pleased. No matter how many times people tell children that you only get something out of life if you put something in, it seems to take at least half a lifetime for that lesson to be learned.

In reality, it is to Gisela's credit that she does all that she does with little complaint except that I need to appreciate it properly. I think I should probably take time to think about that more often.

## 14

# Living together

## *Gisela*

*Financial matters*

There are nine and a half years between Chris and me, and this will, of course, have influenced the dynamics of our relationship. When we moved in together, I was thirty-three and he was twenty-four; I also had three children, the oldest of whom was only eleven years younger than Chris.

Chris's parents were at the time living in Berlin, and they allowed us to live in their house whilst we were looking for one of our own. My first husband, an accountant, had always dealt with the financial affairs of our marriage and so I was as new to these matters as Chris was; I did not really sense any imbalance in the responsibilities of our relationship at the beginning. We had had the provisional offer of a mortgage and one evening the agent arrived to sort out the details. At the time, interest rates were very high, and endowment mortgages were the only things that companies were offering, though it was possible to have a straight repayment one if you asked.

I felt very churlish as I kept questioning whether there was a guarantee that the endowment would pay off the capital of the loan, and the agent was not very clear. He did not actually say that he could not promise that, but continued to do the 'hard sell': in his experience, endowments did do just that and there would be a significant sum left over to spend as we wished. Perhaps the extreme caution of my first husband had rubbed off on me, but I remained unconvinced and even cynical when the agent reassured us that he had an endowment mortgage of his own. He was a very personable young man, and so Chris believed him. I decided that it was important that Chris be responsible for some decisions and hoped for the best; indeed, all the evidence suggested that I was being over-cautious.

On reflection, I think that this was the first occasion that I saw how much Chris will believe the word of someone who, on the face of it, is a 'professional' and is apparently trying to help him.

Having said that, it may be that ten years as a tax inspector dealing with a number of people who, together with their professional representative, are doing everything they can to ensure that I do not know the truth have gradually turned me into someone who is far more questioning than most. Unfortunately for Chris, and my children, the ability to question carefully has extended to home!

Chris does not often initiate conversation and frequently will not tell me things that really he should do. I sometimes feel that he is afraid of me, but given that I constantly question him to check that everything is going well, then I suppose that he is justified in having those fears. I am also aware that I am quick to criticise him if he does something that I am not happy with. Whatever the reason, occasionally Chris has concealed something from me that I have subsequently discovered. He also has the ability of the autist to shut himself off from something unpleasant by throwing himself into his work and then retreating to the computer when he arrives home, or simply by not opening an envelope.

We have separate bank accounts, but the larger direct debits are taken from my account, which in turn receives a large chunk of Chris's monthly salary. Chris spends very little on himself: there are the occasional compact discs, and minor bits of computer equipment, but his large purchases are very rare. However, he does have his own monthly expenditure on travelling and a few other items. Despite that, he seemed unwilling to tell me if he went overdrawn. I would find out by spotting a letter from the bank that did not look like advertising bumf or the monthly statement. There was no reason for him to think that I would be angry, as the answer was simply a transfer from one account to the other, and I could not have accused him of being a spendthrift, because he is not. What did make me cross was the fact that he had not anticipated it and told me so that I could have averted the bank charges. He also received a parking ticket of which I became aware only when an official looking letter arrived threatening action if the fine remained unpaid.

Since then, I have resolved the problem by the simple expedient of opening any post that looks as though it may need attention. Obviously not all people would allow this – though I have not given Chris the option of a choice. However, I try to be selective and open only post that seems relevant to financial matters so that he does retain some privacy.

I have often felt that having responsibility for our financial affairs is unfair but, given my background of tax, then it makes sense that I deal with it.

## House maintenance and cleaning

When we were first considering living together I was astonished to learn that Chris's main reservation about moving in together was my 'housekeeping'. Whilst I could understand this to some extent, I knew that he had never had the responsibilities that I had. It just seemed strange, as normally it is the female in the relationship who is unhappy about the male's unwillingness or inability to take their full share in taking care of the house.

To me, one of the attractions of Chris was that he was not averse to pushing a hoover around, and he also assured me that he did gardening. I knew that his room was kept immaculately and I had seen his room at his parents' house, which was equally neat.

Things started out well: I would take the children up to see their father, and when I reappeared, the house would have been cleaned and tidied. The only disadvantage was that things might have been thrown out that I wanted to keep. I sometimes wonder how much has been lost in this way. We tended to share washing and drying up, and the children had a rota of jobs that they were responsible for – tidying up the sitting room, washing up the breakfast dishes and feeding the cats. Generally this worked well. We did the shopping together and ate together in evenings.

The garden was maintained, just, and after the birth of our son, we had a gardener once a week or fortnight to help out.

Seven years ago, my first husband remarried, and I was no longer able to take the children up to see him; his visits diminished in number, so that we had the children all the time. For me this was a blessing, but it meant that Chris did not have any respite from them, nor did he have the opportunity to do the tidying up to his satisfaction.

Chris and I have different priorities, though having spoken to friends, I can see that other people may have the same priorities as Chris. For me, a clean tidy house comes a long way after happy children – and happy me. In addition, four children and a full-time job, which sometimes involved bringing work home, left little time to waste on housework, and I just did not feel up to doing more than the essentials, which took up a fair amount of time anyway.

Chris's contributions to the house have varied considerably over the years. He has areas that he cleans religiously. The rest of the house will remain untouched. He has never touched the children's bedrooms, and since the early days, our bedroom has been my responsibility. He is unlikely to do jobs that are not weekly, for example cleaning windows, unless I ask him to, so those are normally left to me. He also seems to adopt certain areas for particular attention. The kitchen is a particular favourite, especially the working surfaces. I like the kitchen working surfaces to be clean too, but often by the time Chris arrives home, the rest of us have been here for a couple of hours and there may be a bit of a mess. For several months, Chris would dash into the house, and without a word of greeting get the vacuum cleaner out and hoover the working surfaces. Sometimes, the first I would know he was home would be the roar of the vacuum cleaner as he tackled the kitchen. I would feel that he thought that I should have done it and feel defensive and cross; the start to the evening would be full of tension.

For quite a long time he used to clean the bathroom. I could never understand why it took him at least an hour, when I could do the same in twenty minutes, or why it had to be done on Sunday morning when there was a queue of people needing to use it. However, the responsibility for this seems to have devolved to me, though I think that Chris feels that the children should take a share, which I suppose is not unreasonable.

I sometimes feel that Chris has to see order, than for it to really exist. He is quite happy to tidy up a pile of papers without really doing the work necessary to sort them out and deal with the contents of any correspondence. I would rather leave them in a disorganised pile and eventually get round to doing the complete job.

I know Chris thinks that I am untidy, but I find it surprising that rubbish that is too large to go in the dustbin is just slung outside the back door, meaning that there is a build up of old furniture, cardboard boxes and even electrical equipment there sometimes. I am unable to understand how he is able to look at that without it affecting his Asperger sensibilities, because I can't.

## Gardening

The garden is a mess. The lawn does get mowed when it desperately needs it. This is a job that I prefer not to do unless I have to as I have hay fever. This year, my son and I weeded and tidied the front garden, but the back garden has hardly been touched. Chris really does not appear to like working in the garden, despite what he told me before we moved in together. Yet, if I suggest that he does a specific job, for example mowing the lawn, then he will do it fairly willingly, and I wonder if it is not so much lack of interest in gardening but rather it is not part of his regular routine.

## Decorating

I have done all of the decorating in the house. Chris has helped me occasionally, but it is down to me. He once explained his reluctance because he does not like the less than perfect job that I do. I would really like him to say something that showed appreciation for the work that I have put in on this, but he doesn't unless I suggest that he should. By that time, I have become cross.

## General maintenance

Organisation of this is down to me. Chris is able to deal with electrical problems, but I do wish that he would deal with problems more quickly. I have to sort it out and I find this wide spread of responsibilities a strain, though recently there are signs that this is changing. Chris's father has been a wonderful help on many occasions and I am extremely grateful to him.

## Pets

We have four cats and Chris is wonderful with them. One of them was run over and I heard him crying across the road. Chris came and took over, gently carrying him inside in a blanket and checking him over. I was too much of a coward. Chris also deals with the dead offerings from the night's hunt that they leave, or the prey that make it into the house alive.

## The stepfather

If there is one aspect of my life that I really regret, it is the effect on my three older children of living with a stepfather. It is difficult sometimes to be objective about the effect of Asperger Syndrome. I have no doubt at all that it has significantly affected Chris's ability to form an enduring and mutually satisfying relationship with them, but it is also difficult to be certain of how any man would deal with my particular children. In addition, their father was a very strong presence in their lives for the first five years that Chris and I were together. This benefited the children enormously, and also meant that Chris, quite rightly, took a back seat as he did not want to muscle in. Once a year, John, my ex-husband, came on holiday with us, and while it may have been uncomfortable for Chris, he believed that it was right for the children. Not many men would have agreed to these arrangements, and I know that Chris agreed to them for the right reasons.

All of a sudden, when my first husband remarried, this almost perfect (for the circumstances) arrangement halted. Hugh was fifteen, Henry nearly fourteen and Olivia twelve. I was pretty upset about the alteration in the arrangements and so were the children.

Hugh is quiet and has (nearly) always been very little trouble. I know that Chris has a lot of respect for him and was very sympathetic during Hugh's first term at university. Hugh had gone to university in the absence of anything else that he wanted to do.

Although he coped well with the course and being away from home, Hugh was still not certain that he was happy there and came home at weekends. Chris was extremely understanding and it was never too much trouble to set off at 9:00 or 9:30 on Friday evening, after the traffic on the M25 had died down, to pick Hugh up from university at Royal Holloway. Hugh considered leaving university at the end of the first term, but Chris provided the very sensible advice not to leave until Hugh had used the university's counselling and advice services. As it was, Hugh successfully completed his course and, having graduated, is back at home with us.

When social skills were handed out, Henry and Olivia must have had Chris's share. They have lots of friends and as we live fairly centrally, our house was the obvious meeting place. For me, that has always been a plus. For Chris, it must have been a nightmare; I know that even some people not on the spectrum would dislike the steady troop of friends up the stairs or the chance of finding teenagers in the kitchen. I loved it, and perhaps that was one of the reasons that I have now changed career to become a teacher at secondary school.

If Chris did come across a stray teenager in the kitchen, he would rush through and there was no doubt at all that people found it unnerving. It made me angry, and the children resentful that their friends were made to feel uncomfortable. If Chris is unhappy about something, rather than voicing it openly, he will mutter something under his breath. Hugh, Henry and Olivia are used to a far greater degree of openness. If you want to make a comment, then it is better out and discussed than just hinted at.

To my relief, and the children's credit, they just got on with their life, but it meant that they tended to keep their friends in their bedrooms. Until Olivia left home for university, I was never quite sure which hung-over young woman was going to appear from her bedroom on a Sunday morning.

By this time, Chris was barely exchanging glances with Henry and Olivia, and I did find it upsetting. Ideally I would have preferred some sort of relationship, though at least it was not all-out war as seemed to happen in some families. Generally he would not openly interfere, but would sometimes take action about their untidiness, particularly Henry's, by throwing an item of his that had been left on the bathroom sink, back into Henry's room. If he thought that they were too noisy at night, he would slam a door rather than taking the more adult approach of asking them to keep the noise down a bit.

It was impossible to defend his behaviour and instead, I found myself defending the behaviour of the children, when sometimes Chris may have had a point.

Despite all of this, on our first holiday without the three older children, we drove off the ferry in France, and Chris said: 'It doesn't seem right without them'.

Both Hugh and Olivia now seem to have reached some sort of truce with Chris. Hugh does exchange conversation with him and eats with us. Olivia will exchange pleasantries and understands a fair amount about Asperger Syndrome now that she is studying neuroscience at university. I know that Chris has a great deal of respect for Olivia, and the way she lives her life, and I can only hope that in future years, step grandchildren will provide a base for a better relationship.

However, I do not think that Henry and Chris will ever get on. Chris believes that I am untidy, but the only way to illustrate the state of Henry's room is to picture the worst teenage bedroom that you have ever seen and then imagine it twice as bad. Only then will you start to approach any idea of the horror of the room.

Henry, unlike the other two, did not apply himself at school and so I was constantly subject to calls from his form tutors and head of year. Essentially he was a typical teenager and has never lived anywhere but at home. However, he has many good points. He is very kind, very loving towards his stepbrother George, who hero-worships him (an unsuitable role-model in many ways). He works hard at his job and is generally liked. Henry has driven me to distraction, but he is a very affectionate son. I am certain that any step-parent would have found their patience severely tested and know that even his own father has, at times, been exasperated by him.

Chris cannot see Henry's good points and is unable to stop himself from expressing his disapproval of him through a range of irritating actions rather than just coming straight out with a criticism. Recently Henry pointed out to me that Chris had caused me as much anxiety as he had. And this is precisely what I have told Chris. Henry seems to bring out the worst in Chris and I am unable to make Chris aware of how much his treatment of Henry hurts me. As a result, Henry is the least sympathetic of the children towards Chris.

I have not made matters any easier, in recent years, by discouraging Chris from reprimanding the children, but I feel that as long as he does not have a real relationship with them, any comments that he makes will be ineffective and resented.

# 15

# Parenthood

## *Chris*

I've always found it remarkable that in a professional career, there is often a requirement for a demanding amount of study and examinations, but to become a parent requires no special qualification, no selection and no aptitude for the job. Yet the human damage that can be done by poor parenting far outweighs that which can be done by someone who is merely incompetent in their profession. For the incompetent employee, there is also the threat of unemployment, yet it seems to be a measure of last resort that children should be forcibly removed from their parents.

I came to the job of parenting with no more apparent suitability than anyone else, and no experience except that which I inherited from my own parents.

For most of our life together I was always quite sure that I never wanted to have any children (see Chapter 3 on 'Relationships') although I seem to remember that my opinion softened quite a lot later on, even to the extent that I could even sometimes feel quite enthusiastic about the idea, as long as it was a girl! In any case Gisela called me at work to give me the news that I was to become a father. This was not a planned pregnancy: at the time I was quite ambivalent about it and my colleagues probably thought I was being extremely miserable in not displaying the usual celebratory signs. However, it wasn't long before my mood changed, helped along by the obvious enthusiasm of Gisela's sons and daughter. Naturally for me, there was always a strong temptation to view the whole process of Gisela's pregnancy as an interesting scientific observation, but guidance from her made sure that it didn't go too far.

An early test revealed that there was a slightly increased chance that the baby might have Down syndrome; Gisela underwent an amniocentesis, and so we knew quite early on that the baby was a boy. Despite having felt that I would prefer a girl, it took very little time for this feeling to evaporate. The decision to find out the sex of the baby wasn't a difficult one: we could either have waited to find out that it was a boy, with the possibility of the feeling of preference for a girl growing stronger all the time, and resulting in disappointment at the birth; or we could find out the truth early on and come to some kind of accommodation. In the end this wasn't necessary; the accommodation happened all on its own.

George was always a very active baby and it was often possible to see him kicking. Although this was of course a good sign regarding his health, the major concern I had during the whole of Gisela's pregnancy was that the baby might not be completely healthy, even to the extent that I occasionally wished that the whole business had never started. Added to this was the fact that Gisela's medication is known to cause (although in very limited numbers) facial abnormalities. In any case, the pregnancy was in fact fairly uneventful until the later stages. This is easy for me to say, of course, since I wasn't the one who had to put up with the backache and the enormous swelling, which looked particularly big on Gisela, since she is quite small. Nor was I the one who was forced to sleep somewhere else to avoid disturbing the other partner. This was particularly inconsiderate of me; next time, if there were ever to be a next time, I would be the one to move.

In the last few weeks of Gisela's pregnancy, things started happening all at once. Gisela was sure that the baby would be at least a little early, and of course we had a couple of false alarms which meant visits to the hospital for monitoring, but with no particular result. These visits were quite exciting, because they could have meant the actual start of the birth. As it turned out, one afternoon while I was fixing some shelving in the garage, Gisela decided that we had to go to the hospital because her waters were leaking.

There were no more than twelve hours between our arrival at the hospital at some time in the evening and George's delivery at 6:45 the next morning. I must admit with some regret that those twelve hours have become rather unclear in my memory. At first things seemed to be going rather slowly; there seemed to be nothing wrong with the baby, but not much progress either. In fact one of the doctors had made a mistake, albeit certainly not a serious one, which had helped to hold matters back. Fortunately one of the experienced midwives noticed it, by which time Gisela was so full of oxytocin that everything started happening suddenly and very painfully for Gisela. (Surely if there were no such thing as maternal amnesia the human race would never have got started!) I did what I could to help, but I didn't think it was helping much; even the epidural seemed not to have very much effect, and there were a few miserable hours for both of us, and I wasn't even the one feeling the pain. In hindsight, I suppose that the really difficult period was quite a lot shorter than average, and in fact it was not too long before the delivery itself started. From my inexperienced point of view this seemed to go quite quickly; both the midwife and I were giving Gisela lots of encouragement and sure enough the baby appeared in what seemed like only a few minutes. I regret to have to say that, although this is supposed to be one of life's special moments, I find it difficult to remember feeling any particularly strong emotion. I'm sure that in any case we were both happy to get the whole thing finished. I think Gisela was quite tired at that time; I know I certainly was. I had no special feeling of pride or happiness, or even panic about wondering what to do now. In fact my overwhelming feeling was one of wanting to get some sleep, and so I went back to the room in the hospital where Gisela had been staying, hoping to find a bed there but unfortunately the room was empty...so I slept on the floor for an hour and then went home. Naturally I used most of my time that I was allowed off work at the hospital.

Those feelings of pride started quite shortly after the birth, and I was very keen to show our new baby off to as many people as possible. However, it soon became clear that George was not going to be a great sleeper. My memory of the almost four years it took for him to settle into a regular sleeping pattern was that it would usually be me who took him downstairs to try to settle him and otherwise keep him amused. (My memory might be selective on this point!) It also turned out fairly soon that his preferred place for sleeping was on a beanbag. I don't know what the childcare professionals would have to say about that, but when your nights are regularly and predictably broken for so long then anything which eases the pain is worth doing.

George turned out to be an easy baby to look after: he had no problems with feeding, and he wasn't fretful or prone to crying at the slightest provocation. Despite having occasional ear infections he was in good health. After he settled into a regular sleeping pattern I sometimes caught myself wondering how I could have been so lucky, having heard what a hard time some parents have. He was also a good traveller, and remains so to this day.

I don't subscribe to any particular theories, fashions or fads about how children should be brought up, although naturally I have some opinions about a few things, one of which is that it's absolutely wrong to hit your children. I use the word 'hit' deliberately because whether you call it a tap or a slap, it's still hitting, and it is in fact the use of physical violence against someone much less able to defend himself. Now, although George gave us an easy time throughout his early childhood (except for the sleeping), he could be excessively worried by certain things, since he had obviously inherited some of his father's irrational anxiety; for example, I was frightened of the sound of flushing toilets! I therefore considered it important to try to make sure that George felt as secure and as confident as possible. This is one reason why I don't use violence against him, since it is guaranteed to reduce the feeling of security he should be getting from his parents. If he can't feel secure with his own parents then I'm convinced that it is likely to be damaging. It is also an effective means of ensuring that children grow up learning that violence is a good way of imposing your will on others.

I have always been concerned, perhaps excessively so, with ensuring that George eats a healthy diet. Although we never had any problems with feeding him while he was still a baby, since he has been able to express a choice I think the range of food he eats is quite limited. I know that my level of concern is in fact rather irrational, because if George were lacking some essential vitamin or mineral, he would be ill on a regular basis, which just doesn't happen. However, alongside all the chips and bread he eats I try to make sure that he has a regular intake of fruit and those vegetables which he will eat, which are peas, raw carrots and sometimes even broccoli. George, however, finds my concern a little irritating!

We are not the kind of parents who think they always know best how to educate their child, and tell the school so at every opportunity, and with two teachers in the immediate family we think that, in the main, teaching staff actually know what they are doing when they have the opportunity to use the skills they have. So it was almost as a measure of last resort that we asked George's school for a meeting when it seemed that he had been subject to a certain amount of bullying, and the school appeared to be saying in one of George's reports that, far from making progress, he had actually gone backwards from one year to the next. What was most telling was the fact that, despite knowing George's family history, they had expected him to answer a certain question in a certain way, but George had interpreted the question too literally. Although the answer he gave was in theory correct, it was not the answer they were looking for. We had hoped for a little more flexibility and understanding from the school, especially since they had been told more than once about my own history. We were also not impressed by the school's emphasis on the quality of handwriting and lack of attention to the children's social needs.

George is very much his father's child: as well as the fact that he looks like me, his whole nature is quite similar to mine at a similar age, although with some notable differences. He can be very shy of strangers, uncomfortable with new situations and unfamiliar surroundings, and with an occasional tendency to a lack of politeness, which is quite probably a result of those characteristics. Still I think that overall we have been very lucky with George, if that is the right word. He remains very attached to his parents and loving, with no apparent tendency to want to hide in his own world and keep things hidden, and given the right surroundings, he is quick to learn and be relaxed.

## 16

# Parenthood

## *Gisela*

One night, when we were first going out, we were walking home and Chris stopped to pick up a cat that had rubbed against him. He held the cat closely and brushed his face against it. For some reason I found this very touching; it suggested that he was affectionate, though I have heard since of a person with an autistic spectrum disorder who likes the feeling of their pet's fur on their face. Later, when we were first living together, as we stood in the supermarket checkout queue, Chris would look at small children sitting in the trolleys and it was clear that he liked them.

In fact, George was a happy accident; we had discussed having a child and more or less decided against it, though in retrospect, I think that was probably more my decision than Chris's. But everyone was delighted, and Chris was very proud. At the time I was insistent that he give his parents the news, not me, and furthermore suggested that he tell his parents that he was pleased. So even then, I suppose, I instinctively encouraged Chris to say more than he might have done if left to his own devices.

The memories of my pregnancy with our son are generally happy, and I felt that the whole family were expecting. My older children were excited and would often refer to a book on pregnancy to check the progress of their future sibling, which we discovered halfway through was a boy, whom Chris named George.

Chris, quite unlike my first husband, was fascinated by the pregnancy and his sense of wonder at the process was uplifting. He liked to feel the baby kicking and wanted to know how it felt to be pregnant. He would look at the 'lump' and I never had any sense of him finding me unattractive; in fact, it was quite the opposite, he still made me feel very feminine right throughout the pregnancy.

Chris was less sympathetic to my restlessness at night and it was me who would have to go to the spare bed. At least that was the way it seemed. Looking back, I am sure that had I explained to Chris that some allowances had to be made then he would have made them, provided I had been specific about what was required. He also seemed unsympathetic after I had had an amniocentesis following a blood test, which suggested there was a higher risk than normal of the baby having Down syndrome. He seemed grateful for my children's concern for the unborn baby, but after the amniocentesis, I was supposed to rest for twenty-four hours, and I had hoped for some tender, loving care from Chris. This was not to be; he seemed to see it as a good excuse for having a day off work and I felt a little hurt that he was not more attentive. Now I would tell him what I wanted done, even to the point of saying I wanted some sympathy. Fortunately my children were around and they certainly kept me amused.

During the labour Chris was marvellous. The labour was induced and so it was not easy. For the first part of it, after he had looked over all the equipment, checked my charts and shown an unusual amount of interest in the obstetric side of the situation, Chris sat next to me rubbing my back during contractions. I had to ask him to do this, but I have no doubt that he would have continued all night if I had wanted him to. I sensed a real commitment to doing what was practically required. Between contractions he continued to keep an eye on the equipment in the room, and on the notes on the end of the bed. The contractions became very strong and I opted to have an epidural. I had been managing up to that point with Chris's help and breathing exercises. Whilst the epidural was being set up, I had to lie on my side and during that time the contractions became enormously strong and I lost control and began to cry. Chris slipped out of the room and when he returned, he too had been crying. This is one of the few times that I have seen such visible empathy with me. No one could have done any more than Chris had, and his obvious sadness at his inability to do more was actually very supportive. It saddens me though that he seems to have completely forgotten this moment that meant so much to me.

Almost immediately after George was born, Chris disappeared and (I discovered later) went for a sleep. Though I didn't know where he had disappeared to, I was not unhappy as the nurse brought cups of tea and some toast for the new parents, and so I was able to have both his and my share, which was very welcome. I sometimes think that my pragmatism has helped the marriage considerably.

George was four weeks early, and the hospital were very cautious, which meant that rather than being discharged the day after delivery, I was incarcerated for a week. I hated it; my older three children were at home, and off school. They were looking forward to my returning with their new brother and we were all missing each other. I obtained a temporary release for a couple of hours, and Chris picked me up, but I was very unhappy when he seemed to use this as a rest for himself. I came home to make lunch for everyone. I had wanted to be pampered, but it just didn't happen, though I now realise that I had not given much thought to him, and he had been holding the fort at home for the week, which must have been a strain. However, I am sure that if I had asked Chris to help with the lunch, then he would have done, but I wanted to feel that he could see that I needed looking after, as I had our son only five days previously. Now that I am aware of the diagnosis, I know that Chris is unable to see that and I will ask for 'tender loving care' when I need it, though it is more likely to be 'practical sensible care' than the TLC that most people crave.

Chris didn't buy any flowers or a card or even say anything romantic, but there were enough people around to show their appreciation; in any case, for me, as I love new babies, a healthy new baby was reward enough for labour.

After I arrived home, Chris was prepared to help with the baby, yet when it came to talking to George, he was quite awkward and would simply say over and over 'Hello baby'. This awkwardness resolved pretty quickly when Chris started to sing to George instead. Chris has a lovely singing voice and George regularly heard 'The teddy bears' picnic'. George was a good baby, except for the fact that for the first two years of his life, the only place he would sleep was on a beanbag, and so, eventually, after George stopped breast-feeding, Chris took over and slept downstairs with him. I was amazed that he was prepared to do this, and without complaining, as I had often wondered which creature comfort was most important to Chris: sleep, food or sex.

Yet I should not have been surprised, as it comes back to Chris's essentially practical nature. He would never complain if one of the children needed the toilet on a long car ride: he would simply tell them how long it was until the next service station and ask them if they thought they could wait. If they couldn't, then he just pulled off at the next exit and found a suitable place to stop.

When George was young, it seemed to be my job to pick him up if he was crying, even if I was busy doing something else, such as painting. But, again, in the light of Chris's diagnosis, I can see why it made sense to him for me to pick George up, because generally he would want feeding as soon as he woke up and I was the only one who could do that. However, that still doesn't explain why Chris could not take over doing the job that I had been doing.

On one occasion, Chris dropped George, through not being sufficiently careful. Fortunately, I managed to catch him, but I was very touched by Chris's response. I found him upstairs, sitting in silence; he was devastated that he should have so nearly hurt George, even unintentionally. He seemed to find it difficult to believe that other people could do something like that and took some time to be reassured. The fact that I admitted to having dropped my first son helped and I can remember feeling like Chris looked to be feeling.

As George grew up, he began to develop a fascination for the computer and he spent a lot of time perched on Chris's knee in front of the computer at home. Chris would explain things to him and find him interesting things to look at; needless to say, we must have been one of the first families in the UK to have access to the Internet, so that, well before the age of two, one of George's first sentences was 'W I N press' (to start up Windows).

Both of us are opposed to any form of physical punishment, and Chris has never been tempted to use any. His patience with George is remarkable; recently a friend described him as tender towards George, and that is a very good description, though it can be a clumsy tenderness. It is only now, that George is nine and a half, that Chris has decided he is physically too big to be carried up to bed.

For many years, Chris took George up to bed and stayed with him until he (usually Chris as well) had fallen asleep. Part of the bedtime routine was teeth brushing, and until George could brush his own, Chris would do it for him, and did such a thorough job that he had to be reminded that it was not a surgical procedure.

Chris is also quite strict about George's diet and does not like him to eat 'rubbish', so a system of bargaining came into play: 'You can't have a bag of crisps until you have had an apple.' George has now started to come to me and ask me for food that he thinks may be designated as 'rubbish' rather than ask Chris, or ask Chris for the biscuit or whatever else he wants, saying that he has just eaten a banana (and therefore is entitled to the desired 'naughty food').

Chris can sound abrupt, but George appears to make allowances. He has been aware of Chris's diagnosis since he was five, shortly after the diagnosis was made. He has met a number of children with Asperger Syndrome and understands that the AS means that his father is 'very shy and doesn't face people when he talks to them'. He seems to sense when Chris has been unintentionally abrupt and not take it to heart.

My concern has been that as a role-model for the acquisition of social skills for George, Chris leaves something to be desired. I have pointed out that it is important that he does try particularly hard to remember to sound as though he means it when he says 'please' or 'thank you'. Chris does seem to be prepared to do a lot for George, and I have to say that on more than one occasion, I have used this knowledge in an attempt to alter some aspect of Chris's AS behaviour that I find particularly troublesome. For example, Chris is inclined to leave the television on if someone calls unexpectedly when he is watching a programme that he is interested in. When I first suggested that this was not regarded as good manners, he used headphones instead and sat with his back to the visitor, but I said that I would expect George to videotape the programme in that situation, and so it seemed reasonable that he did too.

It is easy to forget that even where neither partner has AS, there can be an inequality in the level of each parent's contribution to child-rearing. I tend to feel responsible for ensuring that George does his music practice. Admittedly I do have a greater awareness of the sort of level he should be achieving, simply because I have had more children than Chris, but I sometimes wish that Chris could take more responsibility for remembering to tell him to do it. However, I also felt like that with my first husband, who certainly did not have Asperger Syndrome.

George plays the French horn and recently took part in an outdoor 'picnic' concert at the local secondary school. We sat with friends and it was Chris's first experience of being a parent at an occasion like that; afterwards he said simply that he 'wouldn't have missed it for the world'. It is good to see how much pleasure he derives from parenthood and how much of a 'normal' family life is available to him, through his conscientious parenting.

I do look for areas in which father and son can share interests, and when Chris had some roller blades for his birthday, we bought some for George as well. The two of them go out in the evening and skate up and down the footpath outside the house. Chris takes George to the corner where he can practise his turns. When I was returning home in the car one evening it was touching to see Chris making sure that George turned the corner carefully and was safe from flying off into the road, before shooting off up the footpath.

I like teenagers, but I am aware that they can be unreasonable and sometimes wonder how Chris will respond to having his own teenage son. However, I am confident that he will do his best and always have George's best interests in mind and that we will all survive George's adolescence intact. Chris seems particularly good at dealing with George's bad behaviour, usually by asking him to reflect on it and think about what he says. He is very forgiving and encourages George to make amends for any bad behaviour rather than simply seeking out to punish.

The only area in which we do not see eye to eye is the importance of tidiness. I want the first thing that Chris says to George when he comes in to be 'Hello', and not 'Take your bowl through into the kitchen'. There are one or two areas where Chris feels the need to straighten things up; for some reason, the state of George's bed, when he is asleep, is one of those. So before Chris gets into bed himself, he picks the duvet off the sleeping child and shakes it out neatly. It is irksome to watch as to me a neat duvet is not a necessary prerequisite for a night's sleep and George grunts with sleepy annoyance when he is disturbed.

The value that Chris places on having a child was really brought home to me when I asked him if he was envious of his brother, who is very successful at his job, has a very good salary, lots of holidays, *and* a lovely tidy and ordered flat. Chris answered without hesitation: 'No, I have George'. Perhaps it is because George's love for his father is totally unconditional and absolutely deserved.

# 17

# Social life

## *Chris*

While I don't make a habit of dwelling on the problems that come as part of living with AS, I'm not immune from feelings of regret for what might otherwise have been. The one aspect of my life over which I feel most regretful is the fact that I know I have missed out on, and will continue to miss out on, what must account for at least half of the 'value' that people get out of their lives, namely an active social life.

It is not the case that I have no social life at all, but of course it doesn't even vaguely resemble the kind of life which I see many other people enjoying. Mostly my social life consists of fairly low-key events, such as visits to or from individual friends, with the occasional larger gathering. The last one of these that I can remember was the wedding of a friend from university.

I will know within less than a minute of entering a house or room whether or not I'm going to find it a comfortable or uncomfortable experience. I'm sure that I don't do myself any favours here, because putting oneself at ease in such a situation must be a two-way process, which involves making the other people comfortable with you as well as vice versa.

I will describe a couple of occasions which have been less than successful for me.

We were invited to a party at the house of a former colleague of Gisela's, which was to celebrate his moving into his new house. While I knew this colleague quite well, everyone else at the party was a complete stranger to me, but they were all at least acquainted with each other, since they all worked either in the same office or in the same profession. Naturally enough, it seemed to me, everyone except me had this much in common, and of course it seemed to be the main topic of conversation and interaction. This left me feeling at a rather loose end, with no adequate means of getting involved, with no immediate acceptance and no easy way of improving matters. This of course was not only a very uncomfortable situation, it was in fact decidedly distressing and I felt that for myself to remain would be a situation so unenjoyable of the sort that anyone, given the choice, would want to avoid. The result was that I slipped quietly outside and went to sit in the car. Of course Gisela must have been keeping at least some kind of eye on me because she appeared outside a few minutes later. The result was that I went home with the agreement that I would return later to take Gisela home.

The second example concerns an invitation we had to visit some people we know who live quite close. I can't remember the reason for the occasion, but there were a fair number of people, although it couldn't be called a large amount of people. As I wrote above, I knew fairly soon that I wasn't going to enjoy it. Unfortunately, I was hearing opinions expressed with which I profoundly disagreed. I think I'm quite accepting of a range of opinions, but I just can't accept things which seem to me to be unreasonable, prejudiced or just plain stupid, and I will not attempt to accommodate them. I suppose that being open-minded about things means that it's impossible to accept opinions which are not. In any case I found it very difficult to take any meaningful part in the evening's events.

The result was that I just took part in some superficial chat and made my excuses and left, feeling both deeply dissatisfied and morally superior.

Unfortunately, in my opinion, the majority of people seem all too ready to make statements about matters with which they cannot possibly have anything more than the most superficial acquaintance. I am unwilling, indeed unable, to participate in this kind of uninformed non-debate, and naturally I tend to be rather silent when I think I would not know what I'm talking about, with the result that people think I'm just unwilling to speak at all. I also feel it would be seen as impolite to say openly that I'm not prepared to express an opinion on something I know very little about, the implication being that everyone else is at about the same level of understanding as me. This, I feel, is a major cause of my preferring not to mix with people with whom I am unlikely to find anything in common.

The above problem really only applies where the social situation is likely to involve something more than just small talk. In the average party situation, I suffer from just the same problems as anyone else with AS: no ability to engage in 'polite' conversation, apparent lack of interest in anyone else, the appearance of shyness, reluctance to participate, etc. All this is well known and has been fully described in the literature about AS.

One specific problem which I know not only affects me, but also has been described by others with AS or some form of autism is that in a noisy environment, I find it almost impossible to hear what someone is saying, that is, to separate the sound of someone's voice from the background noise. Combined with the general difficulties I have just described, this just adds to the level of distress and anxiety which these social situations produce. In the same way, for me it is almost impossible to concentrate on something, regardless of its importance, in a very noisy environment.

Surprisingly, perhaps, I once went to a meeting of a local autism support group along with Gisela, where we answered the audience's questions. I am told that this was a great success, and I found this a very easy occasion to deal with. This reinforces what I have just said. During this event I had to listen to only one voice at a time and there was no background noise.

At work, there is no pressure to attend any of the after-work events which happen from time to time. In the working environment, I feel I have little difficulty in coping with what is in fact a fairly limited set of interactions, most of which revolve around the requirements of the job. Also all the day-to-day banter which goes on in fact arises from the job, and so I can actually sometimes participate as well.

This all affects our domestic life. It is true that we rarely have several visitors at once; the reasons for this are probably more practical than social, although it is certainly the case that I would not be happy with a group of people who I didn't know. We have had quite a number of people all at once, but then they were all old friends of mine from university. I think that Gisela finds it quite disappointing that she has gone to several events on her own, and I have to admit that this is far from the normal practice. It is also probably true that with some effort on my part, this could change.

Since my parents live very close to us, we naturally have quite a lot of contact with them. This also includes many shared meals, birthdays, anniversaries and so on. However, I don't feel that my relationship with them has improved much beyond what was always a rather arm's-length distance, at least from my point of view; in fact in the years before my diagnosis we probably came quite close to a complete estrangement. Now that the facts have been brought out into the open, at least they are totally accepting (I think) of me but, for myself, I don't feel it will be easy to build a relationship which has little base to it. I spent much of my childhood, after the age of 11, apart from them. So I find that after that period, there remains little for us to share except the superficial details of everyday life, work and other generalities. Although to be fair, our son, their grandson, has brought something very valuable to all of us.

To return to what I said at the beginning of this chapter, I think, for now at least, that there isn't likely to be much improvement beyond what I have described in my social life. No doubt there are techniques and methods to be learned, in order to deal with social occasions, but the point of these techniques is that they are exactly that, and always will be; there will never be any ease or enjoyment to be had from them, and they will never represent what is going on under the external appearance, which is that it is all something to be endured rather then enjoyed. Gisela and I have friends in common, and meeting them is a valuable and enjoyable event, but I can be quite envious of 'normal' people's facility and ease in a whole range of social interactions. To dwell on this point is of course not very productive, and tends to lead to self-pity. There are therefore two ways to approach this particular problem: either to give in to hopelessness or to value what is achievable and concentrate on that.

# 18

# Social life

## *Gisela*

Generally people think of husbands and wives as a couple who do things together and go out together. For us this is not the case and for a long time I did find it upsetting. Over the years, I have realised that there are occasions where it will be far better for both of us if I go alone.

I have no doubt that Chris would like to enjoy a more active social life, but the difficulties in his achieving this cannot be over-stated. Even a fairly small dinner party is problematic and, I expect, exhausting for Chris. Not only does he face the stress of having to engage in small talk, and by that I do not mean inane chatter but the pleasantries that are an essential part of socialising, but also, if there is more than one conversation going on at a time, as frequently happens if there are more than three people present, then it seems that Chris is at a severe disadvantage.

Chris is unable to follow more than one conversation at a time, and if there is any other noise then that makes it difficult for him to keep up with the one that he is engaged in. The non-spectrum person can use their 'mindreading' powers and their abilities to read non-verbal signs to put the fragments of the conversation together and understand the gist of what is being said. The nearest analogy for the person not on the spectrum is to compare it to those awful situations where you are trying to have a conversation with someone and the music is turned up very loud. Small wonder then that at these types of occasions Chris gives up, disappears, and goes to sleep.

It was not until after the diagnosis that I realised that Chris found those social occasions where he would be meeting anyone new stressful. We had been invited to the house warming get-together of a friend whose child was at the same playgroup as George. This was hardly going to be a noisy rave up, just a small gathering of parents, yet minutes before we were due to leave, I found Chris lying on the bed, and for the first time, I was really aware that these situations were the cause of great anxiety for him and I went by myself.

However, I was not always so understanding and the first social occasion at which there was a problem was at an office Christmas party. We were out for a meal at a Greek restaurant and after the meal, which had been disappointing, there was a disco. I was aware that Chris did not like discos, neither do I, but I had assumed that he would put up with it just for an evening. People remained at their tables trying to carry on a conversation. I noticed that Chris was furiously tearing tiny bits of the paper tablecloth and dropping them on the floor; I was cross and thought it was very childish and potentially embarrassing. After all, we all have to go to social occasions that we don't particularly enjoy, but we do at least try to conceal the fact that we are not enjoying them when that is the case. In the end I decided to leave early, though this involved an expensive taxi ride, when we had been promised a lift, and also my missing out on a social occasion that I wanted to be at because I was enjoying the company. I was very unhappy about this, particularly the embarrassment of trying to explain to other people why we were leaving so early. In retrospect, I think that Chris found the occasion at least unpleasant, and more probably, very stressful.

I had observed too, that in large gatherings, Chris did not mingle with other people, but would hover close to me, and tend to disappear if he couldn't see me. The disappearing could mean disappearing completely, together with the car! Some time ago, a friend who knows us both invited us to a house-warming party. I knew one or two of the people there, and was speaking with one of them when the host, whom Chris also knew, asked me where Chris was. I had assumed that he was in the garden, but a search proved fruitless, so I went out to the car, as on previous occasions, he has spent the evening sitting in the car, but the car and Chris had gone. I called him, and I think he was grateful that I wasn't angry, and he was perfectly willing to come and collect me at my convenience. I spent the rest of the evening talking to people I had never met before. I had a lovely time. This had been quite a friendly occasion, but even that is too much for Chris, unless he is at my side all the time.

It was at that party that I realised the obvious answer was just to go to similar social occasions alone, or possibly to take a friend, and this is what I have done ever since. It is far better for both of us: I do not feel that I have to keep a look out to check that Chris is happy and comfortable which means that I am unable to relax, and the pressure is off Chris to go to one of these 'standing around, making small talk' occasions that really seem to be a nightmare for him.

Chris has been open about his diagnosis and people realise why we do things separately, so avoiding gossip of impending divorce. But I have had to adapt; I would see couples at parties, and think that I would like to be half of a 'normal' couple, until fairly recently, when I had spent a very pleasant evening at a retirement party. I suddenly realised that though there were a lot of couples there, very few of them were standing with each other. They had gone to the party together but were enjoying it separately. I knew that I could tell Chris about the aspects that I had enjoyed when I got home, and that I had lost very little by going on my own.

In fact, I enjoy a freedom that many women envy; if I want to go out, then I go out, leaving our young son in the hands of a trusted babysitter – his father. I join whatever group or night class I wish, and do voluntary work that has brought new friends and personal satisfaction.

Social occasions still arise unexpectedly, especially when out shopping. Chris just slips off if I meet an acquaintance, leaving me to chat, though he maintains that is because I never bother to introduce him. I have ceased to feel that it is necessary to cut one of these Saturday morning pleasantries short. I am not sure how Chris feels when he disappears off up another aisle, probably irritated, but we both have needs, and this seems the best way to serve us both.

However, there are many things that Chris and I do enjoy together as a couple. We always enjoy holidays together, and now that my older three children are adults, we sometimes go on holiday with friends, which has worked very well.

We live close to Chris's parents and see a lot of them. Before the diagnosis, when we went to see them, Chris would say very little and usually bury himself in the newspaper, go upstairs to look at his father's computer, or fall asleep. If he fell asleep it was usually in the same room as everyone else, and I used to feel annoyed both that he had gone to sleep and also when he appeared cross that the noise everyone was making was waking him up. Yet somehow I became used to the fact that he would often fall asleep on the floor in the middle of the room, and was rather surprised when my sister seemed put out that Chris had done this in one of her visits.

Since the diagnosis, I have come to appreciate that often he will go to sleep to avoid uncomfortable situations; I have tried to suggest that he go to sleep somewhere else, where it will be more peaceful for him. When we have people to visit, Chris will join us for the meal, and always help make it, but he will often disappear afterwards and do his own thing. Most people know about the AS and this makes it easier for him to slip away without any insensitive questions being asked about his lack of sociability. In any case, I find it far less embarrassing for myself to have him absent rather than sitting silently and apparently ill at ease. However, there are still people who, even though they know of his diagnosis, regard his behaviour as rude. It seems to be impossible for them to understand how frightening it is for Chris to have people in the house. I do sometimes wonder who has the imagination difficulties.

Embarrassment was something of an issue for me at one time if we went out. Invariably it would have been something that I had instigated, so it would involve people that I, rather than Chris, knew. That, of course, made it uncomfortable for him, which he was unable to express. In addition, he is a fiddler. On one occasion we were visiting very longstanding friends of mine. Chris sat himself next to their stereo system and started to put it on, without asking first. Fortunately they were out of the room, so I was able to stop him. Before the diagnosis, I just thought it was strange and discourteous and was embarrassed about it, but it is much easier for me to distance myself from it, now that I realise it is a reflection of his disability. In any case, he is certainly doing no harm, and he is unaware of what is simply a social gaffe. What I find infuriating is that he does not like people to touch *his* music equipment, though that may apply only to my children and their friends.

I no longer feel quite so responsible for explaining away eccentric behaviour that may be construed as rude. If we are going somewhere new, I will try to ensure that Chris is prepared for where we are going, who is going to be there, and what will be happening etc. If necessary, I will also prepare anyone who Chris might end up spending a long time with for the fact that he is less than forthcoming and that if he doesn't smile, they should not read too much into it.

In the past there have been incidents that I found upsetting and embarrassing, though it is easy to see why Chris behaved the way he did. On one instance, we were taking the children into a McDonald's restaurant. There was not room, so we went upstairs, and the door to the seated area was almost at the top of the stairs; someone opened the door and Chris pushed through, of course, without looking at the two people who were trying to come out. One woman turned to the other and made a derogatory remark. I was very angry, but I can now see how difficult that situation must have been for Chris, even though it was an everyday occurrence.

It seems to be the unexpected little problems that lead to these difficulties. Recently, in a supermarket, Chris was unable to push the trolley through the space at the checkout, so he picked it up, held it above his head, and walked through with it, demolishing a chewing gum display as he went. I think that my face must have been *very* expressive, because he said, 'That was a stupid thing to do'. I had to restrain myself from making a very cutting comment, though I would have felt better if I had!

Yet, for many years, Chris had no idea that he had ever embarrassed me, as I embarrassed him. One instance was when I asked him if he wanted to buy some new underwear, and he thought that a passer-by had heard. We clearly have quite different ideas on what sort of behaviour is embarrassing.

Shortly after Chris's diagnosis, we were invited by a local Asperger Syndrome support group to talk about our experiences. The people present were mostly parents of children and adolescents. We gave a short talk, but what the audience were particularly keen on was asking Chris questions. Many of the audience saw it as a way of finding out more about how their own children with Asperger Syndrome felt. After he had finished, he was given thunderous applause and he seemed very surprised. He explained later that he had thought that people were looking forward to seeing somebody falter, or make a fool of themselves. I found this staggering, and I can only wonder at what experiences had led Chris to this pessimistic view of other people, because he certainly does not like to see people fail.

Chris likes quizzes, and about three years ago, a friend asked if we would make up a team with her, her husband, his brother and his partner and another couple. Chris had briefly met my friend, but neither of us knew the other members of the team. It was easy for me, but Chris sat with his chair turned away from the table, almost as though he was not part of the group, though he still took an active part in answering the questions. It was the first time that I really felt that he was different from other people; afterwards, my friend said that her brother-in-law's partner had noticed. Chris is good at quizzes and so he is useful member of the team, and we were invited back to the same team at a different venue. This time, Chris sat facing in to the table, and did not appear to be sitting at the edge of the group, and with each successive quiz, as he has become more familiar with the other team members, he has seemed to relax and even make witty comments.

For Chris, the good thing about taking part in quizzes is that he can be confident of some measure of social success, or at least not feel socially excluded. He knows that he is a valuable member of the team, because of his wide general knowledge. There are occasions where he has done a round almost unassisted: the sea areas around Great Britain is one topic that comes to mind. Having listened to the shipping forecasts for years on end resulted in a maximum score on that round! He is also a walking map of the London Underground, which has proved useful on occasions.

One evening someone came to the door collecting for a charity. Although the collector lives on the same road as we do, I did not know him. However, we struck up and maintained a conversation for about fifteen minutes after he commented on one of our four cats who took the opportunity of the open door to dash into the warmth. I know Chris envies my ability to make conversation with anyone; he thinks it is clever, whereas I am lost in admiration for his ability to converse fluently in other languages. To me, speaking to someone I don't know who comes to the doorstep is no problem at all, but to Chris it is a situation that he really cannot cope with at all. There have been a number of situations where I feel that Chris could have used his languages to do something useful, which I think he would have enjoyed. Sadly his self-esteem is so low, and his confidence so poor socially, that he has lost out on the opportunity because he is unable to speak to people with whom he is not familiar.

At social occasions, he tries to invite friendship by showing that he can do something, and this seems sad because it suggests that he does not feel that he is valued for himself. Certainly the key to a successful social occasion for Chris is to have a purpose to it, rather than just to meet people. Yet he does not seem to appreciate the social aspect as much as I do. We joined a choir that was extremely friendly but very small, and Chris was acutely conscious that the works they had chosen were very ambitious. The singing was far more important to him than the social aspect and he was so worried about being part of an unsuccessful performance that he is unlikely to return. I had hoped that this would be something that we could do together, but sadly it is not.

I do worry that there is a tendency for Chris to sit and not go out. He is a lot happier when we are doing things, and so am I. The real danger of my leading a separate social life is not that I resent it, but if we do less and less together, there is a risk that we will grow apart. This is something that we need to address because neither of us would want that.

# 19

# Employment

## *Gisela*

It may seem strange including a section on employment in a book on relationships, yet employment and money issues are often bones of contention in any marriage. For me, it has been the one issue that, despite my determination to be more understanding, has, at times, seriously affected my respect for and trust of Chris.

I remember reading somewhere that a woman instinctively looks for a permanent mate who will be a good 'provider' for her and her children. In the animal world, the 'catch' is the leader of the pack, and I suppose some of us instinctively move towards someone who appears capable in some way or other. Whilst I certainly do not expect to be 'kept', I would like to be able to get on with my own job, without any anxiety about Chris and his.

I had no reason to suspect that Chris would be anything other than successful at work. He was intelligent, and had been academically successful, though probably not as successful as he should have been. From what he said, he had held various holiday jobs without any problems, and certainly, during the recruitment round at university he had no trouble finding a job. He began work in capacity planning (something to do with computers) for a large multinational, and I joined the Inland Revenue to train as a tax inspector and moved to Watford.

Chris stayed in his first job for a couple of years, and then, without consulting me, he applied for and accepted a job with a utility company that was nearly fifty miles away. At the interview he did not ask about conditions of employment, holidays etc., and the salary was very little more than he had been earning. I was astonished that he had not discussed it with me at all, and that he had failed to ask what I considered to be common-sense questions. The journey was costly and lengthy, and, after I had our son, I became very resentful of the fact that, although we were on the same salary, I was having to deal with the responsibilities of the baby at both ends of the day and he did not seem aware of the difficulties that this caused me, particularly as I did not drive at that time for medical reasons. Chris quite enjoyed the job, but he did not really progress, though that could have been a reflection of the employment situation at the time.

I suggested that he should think ahead about his career, and have some direction; eventually he told me, sitting with his back to me, that he wanted to do medicine, and he had always wanted to do medicine. There was undoubtedly some truth in this; unfortunately, at school, he said, he was not allowed the subject choice at A-level that he wanted, which was French, German and Chemistry. I was taken aback, but certainly not unsympathetic, and said that it was still possible. Yet it was me who found out how he could progress along this path. Because I could understand the attraction of the job, it never occurred to me to press Chris for the reasons that he wanted to do medicine. Chris was not offered a place at his first interview and it was only after he had a further unsuccessful interview at Manchester, where he had done his first degree, that he agreed to practise with me. I started to advise him on interview technique and discovered that the reasons he had for wanting to do medicine were quite different from mine. Or rather, the reasons that he had given at interview were quite different from mine. There is no doubt that Chris has a desire to help people, but the reason he gave for wanting to do medicine was because he knew that he had the ability to do the course. I suggested that that was not a strong answer because his academic history clearly indicated that he could cope with the course; in any case, he would not have been offered an interview if there was any doubt about his ability. I suggested something along the lines of wanting to spend each day feeling that he was doing something to improve the quality of someone's life, and he said that that went without saying, which of course it does not. Sadly, he was also unsuccessful at Newcastle, and he said that he had felt that he sounded monotonous. Throughout the previous two years, he had been attending night classes for two A-levels, Biology and Chemistry, while George was still quite young and not very good at night. Chris did achieve Bs in these, with very little work. I still think it might have helped him in the following year had he done some more work and achieved an A in Chemistry, which he was easily capable of doing. What really surprised me was that he was reluctant to accept advice and seemed relatively unmoved when he wasn't offered a place, though the truth is that he very rarely expresses disappointment, even when he is feeling at rock-bottom.

There are people who believe that people with Asperger Syndrome cannot make good doctors, yet I am certain that Chris would have been a good and conscientious doctor. He would have been thorough and, although he is not a mind-reader, if he knows that someone has a problem, then he wants to do something to resolve it for them. He is ready with the paracetamol, but not so good with the gentle words. And he listens, which is not an ability that all doctors seem to possess.

Chris reapplied the following year, but was not offered an interview, so he had wasted three years and was now thirty. He continued at the same company, and there was one incident that I now
realise was very 'Aspergerish'. Our son was not good at night, and
Chris took the lion's share of dealing with him. Chris likes his
sleep, and has the wonderful ability to be totally refreshed after a
short catnap. Unfortunately, he took the odd catnap at work, sitting
up, in full sight of the other employees. This was eventually
reported to Personnel, who referred him to a doctor for a medical
examination, who of course said nothing was wrong. I was livid; it
seemed common sense to me that you did not fall asleep at your
desk: at best you are a laughing stock, and at worst you can be disci-
plined. Yet Chris could not understand what all the fuss was about;
he observed that the women laughed and talked all day and he
worked much harder than them, which was probably true. On
reflection, I can understand how illogical the objection to his
falling asleep at his desk was. At the time I was disappointed, horri-
fied and unable to understand how he could not appreciate the fact
that laughing and talking were seen as acceptable, but sleeping at
his desk was certainly not. I just tried to understand and made sure
that he was aware that he should not do it again, which he hasn't.

Chris also seemed to make acquaintances at work, and on rare
occasions has invited them back home, or enjoyed trips to the pub,
though very rarely have these acquaintances lasted beyond the job.

I was encouraging Chris again to think ahead, yet he seemed
devoid not only of ambition, but also of any idea of the importance
of ensuring that he at least stood still and did not fall back in the fast
moving computer world in which he worked. However, he eventually started to look elsewhere as it became clear that his department
was to be 'outsourced'. From that point, Chris has suffered from
bad luck and the effects of his Asperger Syndrome that have
severely affected his confidence. I am sure that I have not helped

him with his self-esteem, even though I have helped him in the process of looking for jobs.

He was very happy at his next job, at Tandem Computers, though there was insufficient work. He was giving support to computer users in French, German and on the odd occasion Russian. He worked with a small group of other young men of various nationalities and spent most of the day talking in German. For some reason, he finds communicating in foreign languages easier than English, and I am sure that he has more confidence in himself, because he can be sure that people are impressed with his facility with foreign languages. Any quirks in communication are seen as accidental and the result of slight misunderstanding because he is speaking in a language that is not native to him. The department at Tandem was new and there seemed to be little work to do, which he did not like.

Six months after he joined the company, he came home to show me an email to all employees advising them of what was a completely unanticipated takeover by Compaq. Of course, the announcement was upbeat, but the tone of it suggested immediately to me that the takeover was unlikely to have any advantage for Chris and in fact it seemed potentially bad news. Initially, he did not believe me but decided to look for another job when he realised that there would be nothing at Tandem for him. It is really from there that he seems to have been in a run of misfortune that has been difficult and frustrating for both of us.

He found another job quite easily, though the salary was little more than he had been earning. The job seemed promising, lots of work and plenty of training were promised at interview. However, that was not the case. For three months he again had nothing to do. I was frustrated because I thought that he could at least spend some time studying, but he always seemed to have the idea that training should be provided, which of course it is in better companies.

With very little warning, he was sent to work for a period of time in Dover that became more and more extended and eventually lasted for seven months. His line manager, who was based in Glasgow, did not even recognise Chris on a visit to head office. I think that was when I began to feel a bit desperate about security and the future in the line of computing that he was in. It was clear that the job had a limited lifespan, the project had been poorly led and a couple of managers subsequently lost their jobs. However, Chris took some time to make the decision to move. He seemed totally unaware of the politics of the situation and was inclined to believe whatever anyone told him, if they appeared pleasant. It was also at this time that I began to realise how the Asperger Syndrome was preventing his success at interviews. He was turned down for 'lacking oomph' on one occasion and the reasons given were often similar. What his hesitant and apparently nervous manner belies, of course, is his calm manner in dealing with practical problems. He can have a sense of urgency, but not so that it gets in the way of a logical approach. So while other people may be having a panic, Chris gets his head down and tackles the problem in hand.

I have no fear of interviews at all: I feel a rush as I sit down at the beginning, but after that I quite enjoy them. But for Chris, the whole process is discriminatory. Many jobs routinely ask for good communicators, even if the communication required is technical rather than social. I am fairly successful at interviews, and I some-times wonder if interviews test your ability to say that you can do the job, rather than your ability to actually do it. Chris is fine with the technical questions, and always does well on technical tests, but it is the general questions that pose problems for him, the ones where there is not a logical answer, or where the logical answer is the one that you are not supposed to give. 'Why do you want this job?' The answer, of course, is not 'Because it pays well', but some clichéd response about wishing to meet a challenge or some other inspired platitude. Chris does prepare answers for questions like this, but there is always the chance of questions that you have not considered.

In the past, Chris has found himself at interviews for inappropriate jobs because he either does not think to or is reluctant to ask employment agencies questions about the jobs that they are putting him forward for. The last time Chris was job hunting, I put 'Post it notes' across the top of the computer screen with the questions that he had to ask every agent who called about a job, and this seemed to help.

However, Chris's weakness is initiative and thinking ahead, as I discovered with the job that he took after the 'Dover experience'. He saw a job advertised as the Information Technology manager at a boys' public school and decided to apply for it. I felt sure that it would be a perfect place for him to work. There would be extra-curricular activities in which he could become involved and I thought that he might find people who had more in common with him and his interests, as generally he seemed to have little in common with many of the other people he had worked with.

We looked at the job specification carefully and he was confident that he could deal with the technical requirements of the job. I said that I could advise him on the other aspects, most of which seemed reasonable common sense. I was delighted when he was offered the job, though I realised that he had some reservations but that is not uncommon for anyone starting a new job.

Meanwhile, he returned from Dover to the head office and had another three weeks to serve his notice out. There was nothing at all for him to do despite the fact that he offered, and he found that infuriating. No one seemed to notice whether he was in work or not and so he just left, telling me, when I asked, that he had been given permission to leave before the notice period was up. This sounded perfectly feasible. When his P45 arrived, the company had stopped his salary on the day that he had left. Chris reassured me that he had been given permission, so I contacted the company to find out what had happened to his three weeks' salary, and was extremely embarrassed when I found out what he had done. By this time he had started his new job, so I tried to ring him and was unable to contact him. Rather, he was unwilling to be contacted. When I picked him up at the end of the day, I was angry and made that very clear.

To start with, Chris seemed very happy in his new job; he was late home fairly often, and sometimes this was because he had gone to the pub with colleagues, which was very reassuring. He would tell me about the job, and the people he worked with. There was a lot of technical work over the summer, and the employers seemed very happy that he was prepared to 'get his hands dirty'.

I made some suggestions, chiefly to do with communicating with the teaching staff, and I also encouraged him to start making written plans that were ready to be presented. One of the things that I had noticed was that the school did not have a website and I suggested several times that I thought he should investigate setting one up. He would not respond to these suggestions, and if I repeated them, he would become irritated. Eventually, assuming that everything was fine, I stopped haranguing him.

Five months after he started this job, I left the Inland Revenue to train to be a teacher. I was unaware that there were any real problems at work for Chris; I thought the difficulties lay in getting the job in the first place. The second placement of my postgraduate certificate of education (PGCE) was at a 'difficult' school, where the problems were compounded by an unsatisfactory Ofsted inspection the second week I was there. It was a difficult place to work and morale plummeted following the inspection and report. I did not find the teaching easy, and Chris and I seemed to be growing remote. At the time I thought it was my fault. I was having to deal with children who were difficult during the day, and I just didn't have the emotional energy to go through the hoops necessary to maintain good communication with Chris.

In fact, Chris was increasingly unhappy at work. He was caught between trying to keep the network up and running, including some low quality computers that never functioned adequately, and being responsible for strategic planning. He had been advised that he was not spending sufficient time on the management aspect of his job and had said nothing to me about it at all. I had made the decision not to be involved in his work, and this made it easier for him to hide what was going on. He made the odd comment that I should have investigated fully, rather than dismissing: he felt that people did not acknowledge the work that he did, only the things that he didn't do. On one occasion, he said that he felt he was in a black hole, but I took that to mean that he felt that there was no natural progression from that job, and that he was worried that he would not keep up to date with developments in the computer world.

I remained unaware of his anxieties at work until my daughter's birthday. I had gone into town with her to buy a present, and my mother-in-law rang me to tell me the news that he had left work that day and was not going back. It was a very unpleasant time, and there are aspects of it that have seriously damaged the marriage for me.

The night he finished, I went and stayed with friends. When I came back, it was straight into trying to sort out what was a very sorry situation. I was angry for a number of reasons. I felt that it had been avoidable, either by taking my advice, or by looking earlier for another job. I also felt that I had been let down, because he had not been honest with me. Of course, there was no apology, and for once, I really needed him to do some grovelling, because I was so upset and worried. I also needed to see Chris spending every minute looking for a new job straight away. But he was so inefficient in doing this: he would sometimes spend time going for interviews that were inappropriate because he was reluctant to ask for details. It must have been difficult for him too, but I felt the priority was to get another job as efficiently as possible. A number of good jobs looked promising, but none of them materialised, for a variety of reasons. I also felt that he was not applying himself as hard as he could to passing further exams to support his CV.

Chris did not seem to have a sense of urgency about looking for a job, and I felt that I had to nag him. In addition, he finds interviews very stressful. On one occasion, he had one interview in the morning and one in the afternoon. I tended to try to keep a track on what he was doing and so I rang early in the afternoon to check that he was aware of the time and should be setting off to the second one. There was no reply, from either the landline or his mobile. I left work and rushed home to find him asleep on the floor. Of course, I was angry and very anxious that he should be so apparently careless. He could have gone to sleep with his mobile at hand, in case he received any more calls. Yet somehow, his reaction of annoyance made me feel guilty and therefore more angry and irritated. I am caught between the knowledge that though I can understand the reason behind his actions, it does not diminish the anxiety that they can cause.

My immediate reaction is to think that he is irresponsible, which would be the explanation if it were not for the Asperger Syndrome; it is in dealing with this sort of situation that we could do with some outside help. In many ways, the partner of someone with Asperger Syndrome has to adopt roles that are really not very compatible with those of a wife and lover, a partnership of equals, yet a failure to keep a constant hold on things leads to disaster.

For Chris too, this constant nagging must be demeaning and irritating, but it is difficult to hold back when some of the things that he does are wasteful. He finds it difficult to talk about money, and so would find himself going to interviews for jobs that were simply inappropriate, i.e. he was too highly skilled.

I had a job during the day, and was spending three or four hours every night combing through a website advertising thousands of jobs in computing, to ensure that he applied for many jobs each day rather than the four or five he had been doing before I became involved.

Then one of my children's friends suggested a different field of computing, and I passed this suggestion onto Chris. He was very interested and ultimately this led to the job that he has now that has taken him into a more specialised and intellectually challenging area that should be more satisfying for him. However, I was surprised to find that he was unaware of the job market in the computer industry. The qualification he had at the time had diminished in value.

In the mean time, I had had to give serious consideration to going back to my old job as a tax inspector, just for financial reasons, and I was beginning to feel that life was unfair. There was a serious risk of losing the house if Chris did not sort himself out with another job, and I felt angry about that. I was simply very tired, shocked, disappointed and also very anxious that Chris had been, as I saw it, untruthful to me for six months.

However, it is said that you should 'count your blessings' and there were so many people who helped us at this time that I was able to feel fortunate. I had four healthy children, and the older three were very supportive. Chris's parents gave me not only moral support but also financial help in a most sensitive and tactful way, and I cannot thank them enough for everything that they did for us. His mother also took George and me away for a holiday, which was a great help. One friend rang me every day to check that I was all right, and carried on doing this for several weeks. The husband of a friend whose son also has AS spent time helping Chris with interview techniques and put him in touch with friends of his who might also be able to help. My tutor at university spent an afternoon with me discussing the options for me that enabled me to arrive at a decision about my own future. And of course, there was the couple who took me in and pampered me the night that it all happened.

But what of Chris? His AS means that he is unable to derive much comfort from this sort of support that I enjoy. All he was left with was a nagging wife, and a huge dent to his self-esteem. It was a good six months later that he revealed that if it were not for his new job, life would not have been worth living.

Since then, Chris has completed three further qualifications in the area of computing that he is now working in and really enjoying. The career opportunities are much better and the future looks significantly brighter. It seems to me that the more highly technically qualified, experienced and knowledgeable he can get, the more likely it is he can enjoy a job that demands a high level of technical skill rather than managerial talents.

*20*

# The future

## *Chris*

I have written a lot about the past and the way things work in the present, so what about the future? Perhaps the first thing I should say is that a great deal of thought needs to go into anticipating future needs once children have been identified and diagnosed as having an autistic spectrum disorder. (There also seems to be a lot of evidence that early diagnosis and intervention is the best possible therapy.) Also the long-standing public perception of autistic children as being all totally withdrawn and incapable in any sense of looking after themselves is only a part of the picture. Not only does the thing called 'autism' refer to a whole range, or spectrum, of disability, but all these children have a future as well. Autistic children grow up into autistic adults, and those who can at least make their way in the world with any degree of success may still require some kind of help, just as much as the totally unreachable, mute and intellectually impaired adults.

For myself, I think the future will be very much like the present. The restricted social life, difficulties with interpersonal relationships, precarious employment prospects, arm's-length relationships with the family and so on are all unlikely to change to in any significant way. In my case there was no recognition in my early years that I was anything other than socially timid, no recognition at school that I was anything other than excessively quiet, unsmiling and generally difficult to know and, perhaps fortunately, no recognition amongst my employers (until very recently) that I was unable to exercise a little imagination to go slightly above and beyond the precise, or often not so precise, instructions that I receive. There is also the continuous struggle against self-pity, which, in my case, I seem to be all too ready to concede. I did in fact reveal my diagnosis to my latest employer, and although the matter has never been mentioned in my hearing, I am almost certain that it has been made known to my manager and personnel department, and I am fortunate to have superiors who are sensitive and understanding enough to know when to encourage and when to advise that not everything is perfect, but in such a way that the path always seems to lead to improvement rather than recrimination and blame.

In order to maximise my prospects of remaining in employment which is able to sustain myself and my family in our present lifestyle, I believe that, since I have absolutely no prospect of making headway in a job which demands well-developed social skills, it is my firm responsibility to ensure that I am technically competent, indeed even outstanding, in all the areas of technology in which I am required to work. Given the fast-developing nature of modern technology this is indeed a heavy and potentially time-consuming responsibility. Fortunately, many modern technology manufacturers maintain a programme of technical qualifications, which provide a meaningful target to aim for, and as long as I can maintain these qualifications as well as having relevant experience, then I think that my prospects remain reasonable.

I have no doubt that many of the things I have written here have demonstrated that in some areas there remains a gulf of misunderstanding between us, and perhaps between myself and whoever reads what I have written. I may have intended to create a certain impression, confident in that what I am writing cannot fail to serve my intentions, but yet many readers will come away with something quite different from what I intended. In the midst of this, and the enormous consequent potential for me to do things at home and at work that look completely wrong-headed to everyone else, it is quite clear that there is little or no help available in the United Kingdom for couples or even individuals in our situation. Some kind of regular professional counselling, however uncomfortable it may be at first, where we could be brought together in a neutral situation, and each given individual advice on avoiding past situations and to work towards future improvements, would be enormously valuable. Doubtless however these are not priorities for the National Health Service, and I have myself written that early intervention in childhood offers the best hope for therapy. From this point of view perhaps the prospects for children growing up now are better than they were for me, but there remains a large body of people in difficult relationships who have nothing to rely on but the support of others in the same situation. One only has to look at the number of email forums for partners of people with AS to realise the need for support. One also has to wonder at the patience of the (mainly) women who live with these relationships.

In summary, then, am I optimistic for the future or not? I have already written here that little is likely to change from the way it is now. While there are improvements to be made to our domestic life and arrangements, there is still no prospect of any external professional support, and the range of employers who would even have the faintest idea of how to accommodate an employee like me must be very small indeed. So while I suppose that for someone with AS what I have so far gained out of life could be seen as quite successful, I remain constantly aware that there are many things that remain closed to me.

# 21

# Postscript

## *Gisela*

When Chris and I discussed writing the book, we agreed that we would read and edit each other's contribution. That is, in the interests of avoiding divorce, we should both be satisfied that we were happy with what was published.

This was most certainly not a way of concealing anything that we were ashamed of, or even rather embarrassed about. It was done out of mutual concern and respect.

The book has been written over a period of six or seven months (mostly the latter end of that time) during a time which has not been particularly easy for either of us, and which followed on from a difficult patch in our marriage. This then is a 'warts and all' account.

For me, there are some parts of Chris's narrative that have been revelatory, not least that he does not believe that intimate conversations call for a spontaneous response. To me, spontaneity defines these exchanges. I also was surprised at his description of someone watching over his shoulder; I have felt for a long time that he was afraid of me, when it was really this anonymous being.

I was also taken aback to realise that Chris felt that I did not do my fair share domestically. That is not my perception of things, and I suppose in this way we are typical of many 'normal' marriages.

The final excerpt that I read was Chris's chapter on 'Affection, Sentimentality and Intimacy'. I can think of only one other occasion where Chris has expressed anything similar and that was the day we were married, in the speech he had prepared. It is difficult for me to comment on that section without being sentimental, which, of course, Chris would detest. So all I can say is, 'Thank you Chris, and even if I did have to wait twelve years, it was worth it'.

# Bibliography

Sacks, O. (1995) 'An Anthropologist on Mars.' London: Picador Books.

Attwood, T. (1993) 'Why Does Chris Do That?' London: National Autistic Society.

Frith, U. (1991) 'Autism and Asperger Syndrome.' Cambridge: Cambridge University Press.

Aston, M. (2001) 'The Other Half of Asperger Syndrome' London: National Autistic Society.

Attwood, T. (1998) 'Asperger's Syndrome; A Guide for Parents and Professionals.' London: Jessica Kingsley Publishers.

Holliday Willey, L. (2001) 'Asperger Syndrome in the Family; Redefining Normal.' London: Jessica Kingsley Publishers.

Holliday Willey, L. (1999) 'Pretending to be Normal; Living with Asperger's Syndrome.' London: Jessica Kingsley Publishers.